FLOWERING MALL

FLOWERING MALL

Brandon Brown

ROOF BOOKS
NEW YORK

ISBN: 978-1-931824-48-4
Library of Congress Catalog Card Number: 2012948277

Cover art by Matthew Arnone

Acknowledgments
Thanks so very much to the journals and editors who published this writing.
I am indebited beyond measure to my friends and co-conspirators. That
said, I want to particularly thank Nada Gordon, Michael Gottlieb, Evan
Kennedy, Lauren Levin and Dana Ward for their particularly generous
reading of this work. This book is for Alli and it is dedicated to the memory
of my friend and teacher Stacy Doris, with love and gratitude.

 This book was made possible, in part, with public funds from the New
York State Council on the Arts, a state agency.
NYSCA

Roof Books are distributed by
Small Press Distribution
1341 Seventh Street
Berkeley, CA. 94710-1403
Phone orders: 800-869-7553
www.spdbooks.org

Roof Books are published by
Segue Foundation
300 Bowery
New York, NY 10012
seguefoundation.com

CONTENTS

TO THE READER   *7*

PIG CUPID   *15*

C BAUDELAIRE *LE VAMPIRE*
  11,000% SLOWER   *33*

CORRESPONDENCES   *61*

PARIS DREAM   *75*

FUTURE PERFECT   *87*

FUSEES 22   *107*

TO THE READER

I'm so fucking bored.
So you know it's been
a few hours since the Cialis got
chopped, groomed by the rail,
coaxed into industrial shape. First there's a sting,
spotty sprays of plasma when I huff,
and then? Revolution. Afterwards,
none of us go to work. In my translation of Charles Baudelaire's
poem "To The Reader," I meditate on the contemporary situation
of work and the proliferation of "work without work." That is, I
read "To The Reader" as a reader who's obliged to repeat a
performance structured according to the familiar contours of the
working day, a day determined on the assumption of production,
but one almost devoid of production. I go to a small cell washed
in halogen light for nine hours. One hour a day I am permitted to
stray and graze with the caveat that I return in a timely fashion.
Indeed, according to my masters the one hour ought to be
considered a luxury paid for with the blood of heroic
predecessors. This production without production
results in a formal surveillance, partly engineered by my own
voluntary surrender of content.
I'm talking about
Facebook. I'm talking about the beginning of the poem
"To The Reader." Work appears in the first
stanza as a description of just such
autoenslavement, manacling
our spirits with folly and vice
because we hunger for them.
On Facebook, Geraldine Jackson describes
a burrito-shaped hole in her heart.
She goes to Chipotle but finds that
going to Chipotle tripled the size
of that burrito-shaped lack. Sweaty
murmur. God. I am *so* fucking bored,
which is how you know I'm surrounded
by those closest to me. We're licking
each other's sweat, revolted by the notorious

acidity of simmering Cialis. I'm Starving
Cute Overload. I'm sure many of you dear hostile readers of my
dreams are already feeling a little hesitant about the second
stanza of my translation, since I describe the characters engaged
in the drama of contemporary work in terms of "master" and
"slave." You're thinking, "What is this, 'Daddy' by Sylvia
Plath." You're thinking is he high. Has he been rubbing hash-
covered knives together in the kitchen. But just as there's no
equal sign governing my translation and Baudelaire's poem, I
don't propose an equal sign between the series of historical
catastrophes we subsume under
the episteme "slavery" and the particulars of that tearful
walk through moist acid I and many of my fellows
and sisters undertake each morning. And yet...
It's obvious that community
is Satanic. This translation
wipes the crystallized snot out
of wens in its wens. You
know, when wrinkles
have wrinkles. I turn to talk to my
master, but I find the master to be an
endless serialization of the Prometheus
story. You know the one.
Prometheus is chained to a rock where he
manufactures a very complex, astonishingly
efficient propaganda machine
praising the transcendent value
of chaining oneself to a rock.
Meanwhile Hercules pets fifty
nubile things in a furry hut, showers in Retsina,
very not bored as he lives the life
of a God on earth. Ugh, what
am I talking about? Reading
"To The Reader"
I find myself foam. My
teeth crumble like mints into shredded
glucose. It's sweet. Do you think the devil has a pillow? Do you
care about David Pottruck and Emily Pottruck? Do you think
that David and Emily Pottruck care about you? I wake up in a

drool lagoon and the first thought I have in the morning is will I
be fired by Charles Schwab today? Being an alchemist used to
be the only job one did 24 hours a day. Even when you were
slopping up ferruginous gruels in a bowl off a plank you kept
thinking, "how am I going to turn this thing into gold" and "how
am I going to turn that thing
into gold." Really chewing on that. Emblazoned pillow
whose thread counts blaze. Leisure arson.
You can't burn cereal. I'd worship Satan
if only I weren't so allergic to the monochrome
gloomy sartorial orthodoxy
and Nordic vibrato of its brutal
soundtrack. I'm not talking to a cat, I'm
talking to my reader. My reader,
you suspect that the stanzas of
the poem preserve a secret
anagram. You're getting
Indiana Jones on this shit. Sweaty
decipherment. It dawns on you
that my *oeuvre* seems to itself assert
a missing or deferred *oeuvre* and
this is cognitively opaque or
cognitively opaque-ish. What we do daily we tend to do without
horror. But you know what never stops working? *Olfaction.*
Even and especially when you'd really prefer it to take a break.
Last summer at my birthday party somebody puked in the
bathroom sink and two days later there was still a stench of it.
Barnacles on the pipe coating the plunge to sheer sepsis. There's
a way in which the radical lack of immediate party is the only
way you know that you party and have partied. Last night in
Stephanie's reading she was talking about the "event that hides
the event." Like spraying air freshener in massive quantities
around this tiny bathroom whose mold spores hold their noses,
howling about bad redolence.
Have you ever held blank whiteness
between your pecs? Blowing on the
dice, I watch those bones gradually
become cynical. Someone
starts paying me to dangle out a window

by one toe, tied by string and the overtakeless
grace by which I glide through the mottled
labyrinth of a gutless piñata. If you can't
read it you can't translate it. You know that
all too well, dear reader. I want your ear
so close to my lips you'll be aware I've
had citrus. Gross lactic fireworks display of
mom's milk. Did you like my pantomime?
Did you ever want to throttle a pantomime?
I'm hesitant to reproduce the central image of Baudelaire's fifth
stanza, the "secret pleasure" of the broke rake squeezing and
biting the breasts of an aged prostitute. It suggests as comic what
is essentially awful. Like a mime acting out your worst comment
thread nightmare. BTW Baudelaire rhymes the word for eating
and biting, "mange," with the word for orange, "orange." I want
to see a representation of my own
brain like I want to see a bowl of maggots
stir from torpor and overturn their slimy turpitude.
Do you think Charles Baudelaire's brain looked
like Nietzsche's? Do you think Greg Louganis's
arms would squeeze the seeds out of an orange?
Do you think he would dare to? When I was being
reared in the Sudafedic waste bastion
of rural American fructose culture
they used to show us videos of the lungs of smokers.
They were always very black and awful. Then
they would show you the lungs of a non-smoker
which I guess were better because of being pink
But still they were not, like, inside the human
being who wasn't smoking so that seems like the kind of
purposefully occulted information which even Wikileaks
cannot accommodate. They also showed pictures of the skulls
of kids who put quarters on the train tracks. Don't put
quarters on the train tracks. Things that make you go hm. Things
that make you go (the sound of woesome grieving at staggering
noise.) This stanza was inspired by something I learned reading
commentary on the first five lines of *Iliad*. So one of the first
words in *Iliad* is *oulomenos*, which normally translates as
"wretched" or "woesome." The word is derived from the barely

morphemic sounds of grieving in Greek, which emerge in full
textual apparatus only in tragedy, where their onomatopoetic
vowel sounds are appropriated into the mixed metrics of those
plays. That is, *oulomenos* means something like "that which
makes you go *oileto! Oiiiiillleeeto! Oioioiloiloiloi!* To ululate.
Every language has its stable phonemes to express grief. In
English we say *oh* and *alas*. Sobs crest inside us like the broken,
crazy toilet in *The Conversation* (1974, dir. Francis Ford
Coppola.) In the poem I alternate between "authentic" or genuine
expressive discourse and ironic passages meant to provoke
laughter in you, my salty reader. For example, I talk about the
death of beloved friends and pets as things that make you go (the
sound of woesome grieving at staggering noise) and then I talk
about sending in your tax return but forgetting to include your
student loan interest as a thing that make you go (the sound of
woesome grieving at staggering noise.) When I'm terrified I long
for the corny, but perversely it's the profoundly corny which
most makes me open my mouth and howl with sounds of woe
and grief. In *Iliad* it's a horrible sickness sent by Apollo as
punishment for bad behavior on the part of the sovereign. That
is, the sovereign's brutality has the effect of causing his own
people to suffer painful illness, die on the sand, become
dinner for birds and dogs. Poor *king*. Everybody's uvulas
flickering with o's and l's when our lover falls. Do you think the
destruction of the Vendome Column in 1871 is one of the top 10
historical topplings of monuments? In
my fantasy re-creation plumes of lead seethe
from the scene of its crash like birds
scrambling tyranny. And Jake Gyllenhaal
plays Gaillard, the best socialist cobbler
in a century known for its outstanding socialist
cobblers. Cobblers you'd happily crew with
and plan a coup with. To breathe is recreational.
To deliver the *coup de grace* to a notionally
stable regime would be so satisfying. Still,
all those francs getting dusty in the abandoned
Bank of France…orphaned in heaps
like those kids in, is it Iowa? My plans to commit
great larceny in this life are relatively non-violent

but I do always escape. Then I recline by federated
waters, translating "To The Reader" until cocktails
arrive. How many poems have I written in order to say
I don't want to go to work today? But if you
forgive me, dear reader, your palm fills
of roe later. Lavishly humped on perfectly
toasted bread. A monument to raked
salt. One which the regime of trill scholarship
will not come blow up when power has been appropriated.
Now let me tell you some more about everything
that I have swallowed. How I obtained a swallowship and registered
with a flock of swallows. Graft into a hard herd. Community is
obviously a long look into whatever you're lacking. Wringing hands
over fealty and oaths, petty larcenies. Petters, and the manicured
hands of petters. Sociability gathers as a painting and everybody
who sees it hates it. You can't love something if you can't read it. But
you know that as well, my dear reader, my dear syphilitic reader. My
translation isn't lubricant for the withered flakes of epidermis into
which you shove tongues and beverages. Gulp. If you could hang out
with Charles Baudelaire, which Charles
Baudelaire would you do it with?
On Facebook Anne Boyer cited Charles Baudelaire
as an illustration of the iconic male artist
who refuses to labor, sublimating his own
creative work to the extent that wage labor appears
demonic, the stumbling stone over which his
astonishing artmaking trips and dissipates.
So these guys, what they do, as Anne points
out on Facebook, is defer the responsibility for
wage earning onto the women in their lives. Baudelaire
famously disavows children and wives, but
has this incredibly fucked relationship with
his mom as you know. All his life he writes her
letters, alternating between extreme vitriol
and the dulcified platitudes of a fine son. But
what the letters have in common is they all
ask for money. In return he promises that he's doing
tons of work, that all he does is work. But Baudelaire as you
know is a brooder not a thinker, and brooding loves idleness the

way Long Island Iced Tea loves ice. I love what Anne Boyer
said, and I also want to add that the heroic male artist as lame
and tragic as he is also gets this one thing right, that work *is* the
stumbling stone over which artmaking trips and dissipates. Or
rears out of a long, terrible historical travail which is not yet
spent. And emerges necessarily wearing the *mark of the beast.*
Now this is not as dumb as it sounds, and my translation is not
proposing that there is even some imaginable strata of ideal art
forms which could only be effected by the implementation of
anarchist principles. And yet...
God. I. Am. So. Fucking. Bored.
I think I'd hang out with the Baudelaire
of the late 1840s. We'd be *about* the same
age, and I would love to go smoke opium
at Courbet's house and stroll through the
Latin Quarter afterwards talking about how
I can't feel my fucking legs, Charles or *How pleased*
am I with the purple albatross spreading
its immense feathers over the crest of my
ennui. Or whatever. What's destroyed
the world is the historical fact that a small
group of people have enduringly convinced a much
larger group of people that it is all right
for the small group to own all the land and
yawn so wide that drops of Dom condense
as the honeyed dew from which poetry issues.
The other group disfigures their body
and their wild potentiality. What I'd like to do
is lay in bed with you, my dear reader, all the time. The ninth
stanza of my translation of "To The Reader" essentially recites
an index of all the things I want to do to you, tender reader, and
all the things I'd like you to do to me. When we're lying in bed
or wrapped around a lectern. I don't want a lecture. I want to
smell your snot and whatever your body likes to spray across
the exposed nerve endings somewhat acclimated to a long period of
time untrammeled by finance. The index is alphabetical. Its
scope is comprehensive. Dear reader, pant pant pant. Dear
reader, my translation brays the sounds of satisfaction. Those
sounds so hateful to Charles Baudelaire and everybody else who

loves labor. One of the best things about the toppling of the
Vendome Column is the perfection of its irony, necessary to
revolutionary libidinality going forward. The icon of destruction
and murder can only be blown up with dynamite.
Courbet wanted to merely move it somewhere else
and reinscribe it as a monument to eternal peace. But
Courbet as you know was a silly country bumpkin.
Just like your translator, who shits amidst ticks
in his dreams and drinks mud. I'm watching
a revolution in Egypt and I'm watching it on Facebook.
I'm there with my whole community. I'm sitting
alone in an ergonomic chair especially suited to all-day
sitting. Bored to eructation. Oh my god.
Dear reader, you are me except you never will be.
We'll hunker together, groping flippers,
masticating the salt out of each other's
teardrops. Here we are, squeezing
each other's oranges! Disavowing
the citrus that rages inside the churning
ambivalence in us. My reader,
my homie, my hypocritical cousin.
Yes, I said that we're cousins.
We're satanic cousins!

PIG CUPID

NO FUTURE

for Thom Donovan

In 1977 we surrendered the future
but then it still happened. Going forward felt improvised.
The provisionality was, in part, an illusion
engineered by the faceless masters. You know,
those guys who sometimes have faces. You can see
them in the Metropolitan Museum of Art. Go see
how the Metropolitan Museum of Art is made
up of tiny Metropolitan Museums of Art. The way
bones are made of little bones and twigs contain
a little ash and smoke, a little fire and twig-blood.
There's no future. Although there is friendship
and the bliss of eating seasonal vegetables.
A mess of bronze and serotonin splattered
in grids over the grit of boiled rabbit bones,
themselves made up of tiny rabbit bones.
This is the measured, crazy
way to say there is no future, but there's
art and friends and fucks. I know that my art
is provisional and pathetic. It should be. I make it
hunkered under fluorescent lights,
biting chlorpromazine. Fluorescent lights made up
of tiny fluorescent lights. Half sex, half suicide. All
future. Half seasonal vegetable, half
cyanide. The homeomery
of everyday life and how this is my
drunk and cum-loving nihilism.

STAR WARS

Ugh, I would *never* go to Burning Man in a million
years. You guys have fun with that one. The window
for my going to Burning Man shut tight
in 1983 when I turned five and my cerebral system started
sloughing off the gilt pillars of progress.
Given the Tarkovsky-shot brain death I've suffered
since, I don't need to fiddle mushrooms under a Pepsi
sign in Nevada. What little pop sensibility still fires
bursts via pre-Homeric river-rhythm mimic.
My performance reviews just barely adequate. My prosodies
barely streaming across the scarred surface of a heaving prosthesis.
I'm talking about the Internet, and I'm referring to Burning Man.
Okay, I'll go to Burning Man. So I can blaze in an incendiary, nostalgic
anti-Jacobinism, since Burning Man is a nationalist display of
saturated mores. You know how that band Crass made flyers
in 1978 that read *Germany got Baader-Meinhof, England got
punk?* If I wasn't busy packing the back of my Saab with
psilocybin and Ciroc I'd bend over a Xerox and engrave the
relevant apodosis: *America got Star Wars*. Both Burning Man
and *Star Wars* express something fundamentally true about our
culture. That given the option to ensure the lessening of
worldwide violence in the name of *egalite*, we'd rather burn one
and wallow in the most gloriously degraded archetypal
representations of such violence history has ever considered.
Germany got an organized cell of native revolutionaries
determined to induce true trauma to the ruling classes and
engage the sympathy of the ruled. England's youth, poor or
bourgeois, faced a bifurcation by which choice was demanded
between fealty to the party of order and devotion to
insurrectionary art. In the United States, if you were white and
loaded and could tear yourself away from listening to Fleetwood
Mac's catastrophic LP *Rumors* for three hours you were most
likely either watching *Star Wars* or waiting in line to watch *Star Wars*.
I know you think this is an empty and raunchy satire. Actually,
like every other white and wealthy person born between 1958 and now
I'm deeply, disarmingly, madly in love with *Star Wars*. *Rumors* too.

CAT, CAT, and CATS

I've often thought that noxious, disgusting animals were,
perhaps, merely the coming to life in bodily form of man's evil thoughts.
—Baudelaire

I'm cutting words into my midriff. Large and Old
English: **CATS**. When my heart jumps inside my midriff
the lungs are its pillows. Cushion for the pushin'. So if I cash
in my portion, nothing's gonna cut into my fortune.
We've got to be fair to the very rich. Their generosity
makes this prosody possible. So I can make a mess of tempo,
overtype into oblivion the mewl of my coterie,
itself blustering from an abyss. Cutting off the price
tag. Cutting off the catnip, the delight in catnip,
the catnip-provoked rassle round. Followed by a
catnap. Everything got so vulnerable-ish. Precarity
from which, I dunno, I'd rather lick the pus out of my
social trauma. Puss in my favorite boots running out
of canvas. General Bonkers. The whole war machine
declares general war on string, so why am I
composing free encomia in praise of string? A chat
(yawn) feeling more like a yarn. I'm trying to read
what my kitten's written but it's all cat scratch.
At the bar Evan asks what am I writing? I say I'm translating
Baudelaire's poems: cat, cat, and cats. He tells me about a friend
in France who heard her cat back home had died and cried and
when someone asked her what's wrong she said "ma chat est
mort," which by virtue of a misused possessive meant "my cunt
is dead." I want to tell you this so we can both recall our pleasure
in one of Ali's opening lines in *Ali: Fear Eats the Soul* (1974,
dir. Rainer Werner Fassbinder), when the girl asks Ali why he
doesn't want to fuck and he says *schwanz kaput*. My dick is
broke. My pussy's dead. I know you'd laugh, but in the
humorless terrordome of chat-abyss I'm bereft of those tonsular
gestures which coax. Good morning baby. Good morning
baby. Good morning Alli. Morning baby. Good
morning baby. Good morning peanut. Morning
baby. I had a chat in my chamber, me in all my snuggery.

General Bonkers wiping his mustache on my whiskers. I mean
real haptic pattycake of our faces. Our minds merged
and I heard the meow erupt inside me. Bubbling like
a cholera which I could not chat away I mean
which I could not chase away. When I am old
and full of paranoia, I'll comb through these chats
looking for gnats, recalling that in my life, before
total psychic disability prevented my holes from
liking to bump up against these other holes
I groomed and I was marvelously groomed.
Someone starts paying me for playing
with my bad-faith allegorical fuck-buddy. Butting
paws and with many flicks of the cutest-ever
button nostrils akimbo we meet in the neutral
zone of spayed intimacy. Click click click. Lick lick
lick. Purr purr purr. Dumped cat in the furnace
meows upward. It's so "resume ready." What
I'm good at is chatter and curiosity.
That very thing goes about killing cats famously.
Cat curling up on a bed of mottled lice. Tonguing
tuna. Zonin' on Ambien for cats. Dreaming of tuna
and crabs, lining up for bottomless consumption.
This is what it's like, when the working day crashed
but we clip our fur daily. Cat pulling a plow. Plow typing into
the fields. I am typing. My typing wrecks of itself. My typing
somehow responsible for dead cats. For the death of a litter
of kittens. Someone pays me to do this.

THE WINDHOVER 2

for DZB and LW

I wake up with a cell phone strapped
to the little buds of me. And then vibrate
down Valencia to the train
like John Travolta in the amazing opening sequence of *Saturday Night
Fever* (1977, dir. John Badham.) Which is to say I
retranslate the urban space through which my kidneys jitter in
order to stage an upset grand in intention, minimal in bird
stirring. And you're right to wonder, if *this* is the maximal erotic
varnish of my vision for the redemption of urban abyss, what
kind of wastrel revolution awaits us in the discotheque?
Rain in May. So unseasonal, as if dolphins
held the reins and, finding our socius indigestible,
schemed to moisten cracker staleness. I accidentally salute fellow
honkies hustling through it. I wrote fifty
reams of verse. I wrote 5…I
wrote five hundred rhythms on paper,
dilating a roll through coal I once made. Abject *hajj*
I made through hay to ask one puny question
of a slick, dancing, momentary guru: how deep is your love?
Pinching the ribs of my briefs and stuffing
as many cell phones as I could to cup glimmering
portals. My heart stirred for a bird, but the sky
stayed soggy, beakless. In its place will.i.am disembarked from a
helicopter at halftime.
My love is deep. It has a history
of shedding gristle and brine. will.i.am parses
the clear Dallasean sky with a message from the future.
It is on the tip of my tongue but it's not something I can *say*.

SWANS

I've got $300,000 in speculative futures and this
is my last monster poem. I'm cashing in, going to Lake Merritt
and laying in the grasses. Fine with the dog shit on my loafers.
In *luv* with swan shit on my glasses. I'm surrounded
by the ghostly voices of peasants displaced so Lake
Merritt could wash their thresholds. Where their beds lay
now loiter mussels. It's tough to be a peasant and try
to camp in the center of financially charged orgiastic development.
J'ai vu le cygnet et il m'a ouvert les yeux. I saw
a swan. I've got beaucoup shares of British Petroleum and 300,
000,000,000,000,000,000
lyric poems cobbling inside my
diaphragm and not one is grotesque
or monstrous. Squatting by this gleaming slag of avian shit it's
cool. Clacking kayaks. Thumping cardiovasculars. The fame
of my monster poems leads me to reflect that I am one
of the top 20-25 monster poets of all the Internet. I stop
to pant, fix my cravat, stunt by the mob of swans at the lake's edge.
Then I read the *writing on the sign:*
WELCOME TO LAKE MERRITT
HOME OF THE LAKE MERRITT MONSTER

PIGS

I would never hold hands with a pig.
But as a vitamin-deprived crackerlet,
my rearers were obsessed with a symbolic play
in which the little stubs hanging off my palms
were pigs. Doing typical pig shit too.
Going to the market. Gumming roast beef.
Slurping trash out of a trough like it was lamb
kidneys in shallot sauce. Sure, I season
my own shapeless chemical dinners with a
little pork product. Inhaling sodium ennui glutamate.
Listening to the lachrymose squeals of an angered
Kardashian, *luving* its peal across the bereft
orchard of my machinery. And I am going to
call a pig a fucking pig. This blonde Franz-type
stalks the halls of my office building.
He nods up with his whole cleft so I can see
the breezy blonde hairs inside his snout shake.
Sparkling honky eyes. He licks his lips
spying spine. Hot lard for a cold
baton. Wild boars still roam the woods
of Marin, but in the streets of Oakland
all you can see are pigs. Saying something sort of
shitty to a garbage collector. I got a ticket for effusive
dumping and the pig thanked me, handing
over carbon copy. Smudging my enduring
dermal affability. I grabbed his tail and pulled
it Botox taut. That's not
compost staining the wrinkles in my fingers, pig.
It's what degrades this beautiful salt-lick
I put clothes on every day: white but pig-hating,
full of lovable rancor. It smells a little yesterday.
Backdated fish. Big potato. What goes
in the garbage. Cognac for pigs

PIGS 2: BIRTHDAY WHISKERS

I recognize myself in the fiscal now
as a wrinkling pleather-face psycho entrenched deep
in the woods of a gentrifying neighborhood.
And it's *my birthday*.
The neighborhood is not only of the mind
but of the geist and outfits. I went out sockless in white loafers,
brown khakis, a pink shirt with a long pick Mackintosh,
dandiacal cravat, brown glasses, buzzed head, and extravagant
mustache, a coiffure sung by one who sings in glory
like in the *Bhagavad Gita*. Seers practice austerities in the
bushes owned by the Arjunas of the Earth
but I'm loathe to deny any pleasure,
a perpetual birthday present to myself and Ted
and Carrie and Mick Jones. Long-lingering
looks from dudes over chalky crepes.
Alli says it's the mustache. But pigs
don't wear pleather. Once I saw two on horseback
outside the Stonewall hesitating
to break up a brawl on the sidewalk. The brawlers brawled
and pummeled. Historical forms penetrate the inns pigs
patrol. Saddles made of cows, draped
across the backs of horses. Cops made of bacon, draped
across the saddles made of cows. The wicked
farmhouse owned by Arjuna is where I live
and into which I have seduced oh so many co-eds
with this docile-looking mustache
into a warped gastric economy. Eat me if you want,
you pleather-faced perfectly-groomed anti-Vishnu.
Jerking open the rusty door of an icebox. Devoted
reader of my works. Happy birthday Ted.
Happy birthday Carrie Mick Myself.

KANYE WEST'S 12,149th OUTFIT

Like trousers, like brain —Joe Strummer

There are two things I can't figure out.
How to disarm this death-machine I'm helping
drive, and how to read Kanye West's 12,149th outfit.
Are these two things finally identical? I've been using swag
to intervene in the signifying regime
by which desire fronts in the cut of my lapels.
You try to read it but sometimes the meanings are beyond you.
Then I have to screed against your ill translations. Thanks.
If you can read English you can sort of read the French of
Baudelaire even if you don't know French, but you cannot read
Icelandic. Although anyone can walk around in an outstanding
wool Icelandic sweater and the allegory of their desire is
obvious: to gouge stubborn chunks of whale sashimi out of one's
braces, drinking through a darkened afternoon
with a patronry white as whale teeth. In *Salon of 1846*,
Baudelaire describes his social class by describing their outfits.
Poetical cravats and funeral habits. So no wonder you'd have to
spend two hours at your *toilette.* You had to stunt for the
kaffeeklatch and the stewards at the opium den *and* enunciate a
critique of the bourgeois monarchy. Aristotle knew that stunting
is a habit. I'm combing through neckwear to
articulate how bad I want this death-machine to
sputter and careen. I'll fall out of it like an oaf
wedged inside a clown car, pale butt in bad britches. Rolling
around in a ditch, wiping tears off my phone. Nobody will mistake
the meaning of my laundered sculpture.
Guess what happens when Kanye West wears a *keffiyah*
intertwined with strands of softest gold? Guess what happens
when Janet Jackson wears a dress
from 2034 in 2002? Guess what happens when I put on saucy
polyester and parade around a diner in ye olde hometown?
I have never wanted to pierce the eye of an old white
Midwestern man with a dagger exactly, but I have wanted
to charge my Jesus piece so hard that my beloved friends
who have left the earth come back—to help me dumpster

dive portraits of Kanye West on vacation in Iceland,
rewriting the sagas. Shit, re*living* the sagas.

KANYE WEST'S 13,522nd OUTFIT

I started reading the *Commedia* wearing Armani and I found that
I could read Italian with total fluency. Clothes make
the subject after all. Bee in my bonnet.
Creased copy of *Commedia* in the secret
pockets of this cherubic pewter blazer,
which I offset with a blood-red cravat
as if I were trying to get fired from a newspaper
in Dijon in 1850. Or any epoch that brandishes
bloody ordure as an accessory. My coven
crumbles and swarms into new patterns. I put some of them in
hell, some in Dijon, and a few get to eat at my table. Those who
eat at my table eat fucking *well.* Licking schmaltz off their
snouts and wiping it on Armani napkins. But then all the realms
seem to be the same. One sadly carved inside a cave inside the
hell of social fondling. I collect bitter letters expressing
resentment that I get to be the treasurer of the coven this
summer. Endless reiterations of fruitless hateration. I ask Kanye
West what he thinks. He's quiet
but cracks canines on a pretzel filled with
foie gras and does not spill a crumb.
I think I understand. Was the noise of his
chewing…in *Italian?* When I disrobe I have
to rely on translations again. On
repentless wizards braced for an eternally
bubbling antiparty. Wizards in weirdest
threads. The hell I help write
is shaped like couture so haute
it makes your large intestine sweat.
Heart on somebody's lapel, bee in somebody's bonnet.
I've got exactly fourteen enemies.
A perfect number to start writing *secret sonnets.*

THE FATELESS

Sometimes I think I'm in *luv* with astrology.
A dance amidst what's too hot to touch, or too hot-ish,
arriving at an oracular pronouncement. Based on which
5,000 years later I woo my future wifey in the kitchen
Inside nostalgia is *algos,* real psychic woe only utterable
by poems but no less painful thereby.
The stars are so mateless we wince on their behalf
and give them names and conspiracies. Reasons to
live. So no wonder we go there when our genius
emulsifies and the bones lukewarm.
The gaze goes upward. An ocular clench
as if in a grimace one feels pain both literal
and fantastic. Oneiric maintenance obscures the
pinch into one's flesh of fetters no less real
for a general absence of iron ore. Socrates
writes a bunch of poems on death row and appropriates
the appurtenances of ancient prison protocol so to wax
on categorical pleasure and pain. @ the slave that cast
those chains *#brush those sparks off your welding mask dude.*
If you brush up against a star it's going to burn a
bit. Aggravating hypostasy of praxis. It's like reality
television stars. So you find your mouth
saying "they're so facile." "They're so aggravating."
"They're so fucking lame," those stars of urban banality. Is this
hotel pager-friendly? Is this lyric beeping too loudly
or too loudly-ish? When I wail I want recompense. I want
sidereal shift and real cessation of global pain.
Not solaced enough by temporary balms—
poems and porter. *Whatever…* This is exactly the ambivalence about
which I like things inside a column of shit. I do like them.
If this is code, it gets embroidered at a Starbucks in Paso Robles,
surrounded by motoring whites who do
not dissipate, except for minutes at a time to excrete
waste and buy runny fruit from baristas. Runny fruit
with a devastating secret. Battered about
by winds barely visible on a night with absolutely no
stars. I mean a day punctuated by strays, moaning

at the buffalo herd behind the fence. Brush those sparks
off your beards dudes. Yip yip yip. Red Gucci sweater,
dice roller. I am so in *luv* with Christmas even dogs
seem covetable or covetable-ish. My tights are snug
because I want you to see everything that I process. Turn
those starlights on so bright. Strobe lights. Flares. Lighters. Give
me a fortune I can really handle. I promise I won't
squander it like some 21st century meth-freaked Charles Baudelaire.
I'll be the utmost heir in tight-fitting leotard
and I will break the yoke on the steel stairs,
admitting the radiance of athletic competition into the
ring from which it spills. In decadently difficult
Indo-European meters. Or Indo-European-ish.
A grimace is not a scream. Napalm is not a chain. In my pocket
I have fabric lint and a credit card emblazoned with the American flag.
With my credit card I can buy Frappucino. It's so meaningful
to eat! And yet so meaningless to extract
dew from the flowers, rub it in between my feet
until honey squirts out. To stride through early
rain in suede, to check my swag in the window
emblazoned with whatever holiday accoutrement
is most critically imminent. Beneath tinsel and insignia
of Santa I adjust the knot about my clavicles.
I do this for a dream about bullion, to show you
what's in the innerest caverns of the
femur. How lusciously it masticates one's native
language. Like baloney I contain an erased birthplace
which nevertheless equips with tours.
And they will make you nauseous. The baloney is my poetry,
and that will also make you nauseous. Bologna
is in Italy. All the speeches I've ever slobbered at the afterparties
resound in this moment. They ruin the ambience
of steaming cream and the sound of boxes,
torn open for their beany guts. My writing
has been awful, tasteless. Fateless. Cherry fish grunt blonde
mastiff fricatives.
What freaks is finally what endures.
I made my wifey cry at a poetry reading and then afterwards
sold chapbooks. And scooped the dead

beta fish and let it cure beneath the mistletoe. All
because everything got so suddenly baseless. Or baseless-ish?
The paeans of Indo-European rhythms disarm the faceless
retinue lording over everyday life, a pathetic armature. This poem,
in blame of the silk screened American flag upon the
credit card in my pocket, sheds no or little light.
And yet what hums more championly
than the groove pruning one's room while watching
Dancing With The Stars? I have seen
the real face of Santa and it is a satisfied,
philanthropic face. Fat on its own tax. Reeking
of a night drinking too much milk by a smoking
chimney. A night of drinking too much cookie
when one has finds one has no toothpaste. I sat on his
squirming, burdened lap. I said Santa
what I want is *fate.*

CREATURE TERROR

What does it mean that my papa's sleeping
in a pool of puke in the snow? Our neighbors
have turkey legs in their claws and turkey
skin in their teeth. I'm fucking in
some straw, learning how to discorset.
No discourse redeems the 4th rate
Nine Inch Nails cover band who dispassionately
rocks this village. We party because
we killed a wolf, scourge of the village
and oh so many corsets. We exterminated the
peripheral lupine community, capping
stakes with wolf skulls to celebrate,
bounce it over dancers. But there is more than
one animal invader in our commune.

When will I ever expel the pig in me?
My house sways. Wolf breath outside
makes the straw shiver. Or is it *inside?*
I date my infection to the late 1970s. Ronald
Reagan got pus on his lips. Mark Paul Gosselaar
drools from his septum. I drape a red cape
over my cummerbund but that won't hide how
bad I want to motorboat a trough.
Would I roll you under a tank, comrade,
for a shot at whatever stew dreadlock
grandma's got burbling over those hot sticks?
Would you let me drown in the river Styx
if it meant a smorgasbord of delish trash for you?
The really scary thing is oink. I'm
oink giving oink

C BAUDELAIRE *LE VAMPIRE* 11,000% SLOWER

A vampire novel for Leslie Scalapino

The flaneur thus becomes extinct only by exploding into a myriad of forms, the phenomenological characteristics of which, no matter how new they may appear, continue to bear his traces…this is the 'truth' of the flaneur, more visible in his afterlife than in his flourishing.—Susan Buck-Morss

Capital is dead labor, which, vampire-like, lives only by sucking living labor, and lives the more, the more labor it sucks.—Marx

CHAPTER ONE *ARCTIC SUMMER*

I've spent the whole summer, one of the coldest ever in San Francisco, sitting in my bed watching the history of vampire cinema on my Mac. A spider has been suspended outside my window, its web stretching in the space between two apartment buildings. It's grown fat and ruddy and I've never seen it move, just suspend, and I imagine it's at least marginally interested in vampire cinema *being evil*. It like Renfield believes that *blood is life* and although the image of Renfield in the asylum eating spiders like some kind of hard gelatinous movie candy must be awkward; I've never heard the wrung groan weep through the window. Still, what a dick, to consume its companionship and meanwhile project its own predator, night after night, bumping the mad shrieks of arachnid hunger. In Dreyer, in Murnau, even in *Buffy the Vampire Slayer* when Dracula comes to Sunnydale and makes Xander his spider-eating minion.

It feels disappointing that this is the summer in which I bid farewell to youth. Shouldn't hot sun be out twenty hours a day to herald my descent into ash, searing the freckles off my haunches which I brandish always like pale, nasty stakes? Wonky left eye of Bela Lugosi. Vampire Miley and I howling *my hands up / they're playing my song* into perpetuity, or until the lights snap off. You know how Count Dracula says to Jonathan, "I seek not gaiety or mirth…I am no longer young. And my heart, through weary years of mourning over the dead, is not attuned to youth?" Well I fucking *do* seek gaiety and mirth. Bring it. This time without the youth.

All summer long I sat amidst decapitated heads, wooing them with bagels at the gloomy food court where we while. This alone appears rigorous in the overtakelessness of perpetual youth. And then my mom wrote a love letter to the food court in which I finally die in the future:

> "Dear future perfect, I'm writing to say *hi honey* and acknowledge your having completed the brutal death of this thing I should have aborted in Missouri. All he did was consume 14,034 beverages and countless carbs, grow in sloth among the severed heads of all his friends and wallow in his own debt, wrenching his hose over and over and over while

his sisters and fellows groaned in pain around him; they went day in and day out to their jobs as coffin-movers at the Panda Express / Orange Julius combo known as the *Pandius*. What did he ever do?

Love, Mrs. Baudelaire"

CHAPTER TWO *MY LIFE BEFORE THE BITE*

I was born a small stain on the flowering wane of a Fordist universe
spreading turkey vulture wings as it slid from a tottering apex. This
happened in Missouri. Born in Missouri in a blue duplex, and I browsed
among weeds and gave them names. Born to rut and spend in cycles. I do
this on bicycles. I shame a barista for making everything too flammable. Too
easy to wreck on one's bicycle. This morning at the café I ordered and
devoured three bagels and then watched the severed heads of my friends
recur as content. Then went back down to the café. They were tapping nails
into a poster with my photo on it. The poster declaimed me an insatiable
glutton for partially hydrogenated hemoglobin. I *really* gave them shit now,
meanwhile bought five Danish of assorted fillings and engaged them.

I was born a small stain on the flowering wane of a Fordist universe…and
sometimes I die and rise from the dead and go out for dinner. I do this as a
poet, having transformed my bed into a coffin, covering it with lush purple
fabric and pictures of Justin Bieber, his tremendous hair. Like the lost jewels
of ancient Palmyra, those unearthed pearls reeking in the crypts of
Sunnydale for me to root out like a truffle-finding pig. How spectacularly
cruel it is to make a pig sniff out the truffles whose destination is a ham.
How odd to make an otter play a shark, to make Charles Baudelaire play an
impoverished, gonorrheal Lord Byron. To look into a mirror and say, "I think
this mirror is sad."

When I kiss anyone's lips I kiss the petrified relics of my initial erotic
yearnings. That is, I kiss my mom. As I lick the sides of your mouth to
suggest my desire to lick your clit until you simultaneously clench and shout
I'm actually Frenching the splayed airbrushed post mortems in my father's
Playboys, those versions of my mom which provoked the initial attempts at
autoasphyxiation and stargazing. I slick my tongue underneath your teeth,
and it's still the teeth of steam that resuscitated my message into my
childhood mirror. Not having any reflection of my own, I traced *I love Sammi*
and then wiped it clean. The sneaky, libidinal satisfaction of obliterating my
own creations. Flushing the "stinky present." Later my siblings read the
message as it returned in the steam and their barbs tore into my cape,
making that nectar lap linoleum. In the caverns where I plied a wicked
auto-acupuncture. A useful lesson for my later life as the undead: there are
things worse than death…like *photosynthesis*.

CHAPTER THREE *GET DRUNK!*

Unless you're a poet or an otter or something supernatural /
you'll drown dear.   —Jack Spicer

In Baudelaire's "Enivrez-vous!" the poem exhorts its reader to "always be drunk." But this can be a drunkenness without drinking, as the poem affirms back: "on wine, on virtue, on whatever." The reason to be drunk at all times, even drunk-without-drinking, is to avoid becoming the "martyred slaves of Time."

Drunkenness will not help the vampire. Though the vampire has a ceaseless need to drink, they achieve the inverse of Baudelaire's exhortation: despite having to drink they never become drunk. Joyce walks into Angel's mansion to try and talk to him straight about his relationship with Buffy. He welcomes her, in an already ironic inversion of the vampire-on-the-threshold figure, and invites her in, saying "I'm sorry, I don't have any coffee." She says, "Oh. You don't drink….*beverages.*"

How Samuel Taylor Coleridge would it be to think this quality of drunkenness-without-drinking as a temporal intervention into emotional apperception? To be drunk while sober means, more or less, to act irrespective of reflective sorrow and installed expectation. I often experience this drunkenness when I am on vacation in another city or vacation in my own city, wandering without plan, inflected by an index of potential directions and encounters, conjugated by text messages or phone calls or bumpings into on the street. A logic of drift emerges as if on plains.

In some Eastern European vampire traditions living alcoholics often become vampires. A replication of that insatiability in the land of the dead. But the vampire is never represented as an alcoholic despite the connection with extreme thirst. There are things worse than death…like *fizzy water.* Drusilla in *Buffy The Vampire Slayer* can be read as the object of medicalized psychiatry, perhaps her spacey and listless cruelty in all its breeziness reminds one of the zoned out opiate addict, but she's no drunk. If you're not a poet or an otter or something supernatural, you'll drown.

CHAPTER FOUR *THE FLANEUR*

Regular flaneurs walk in daylight, but the vampire is the flaneur of the night. In *Arcades Project,* Benjamin describes the flaneur as possessing the "spirit of noctambulism." Angel wanders around Sunnydale after the sun has gone down. But his activities, especially before his revelation as a vampire to Buffy, resemble Benjamin's description of the already obsolete flaneur. Angel was born in 1757, in Europe, and could have easily learned flanerie first hand from those "botanists of the sidewalk."

Twenty four hour Subway. Scraping foam from chopped green peppers off my uvula. My daytime flanerie occurs among the severed heads of my friends; they shout, they tweet and re-tweet, they express themselves citationally. My nighttime flanerie is mostly pornography. The exploits and tunneling vision of country dick and panting on headphones. The spider hanging outside the window probably prefers the porn to Dreyer but there's no way to be sure. My daytime flanerie, rootless among nocturnal flowers whose consensus is wishing flies flew at night. The consensus for nighttime is Subway's okay. Animated sandwich in the form of a boy between two boards. A boy himself eating a sandwich. His otter skin actuates my saliva glands. And I *would* eat a sea otter sandwich. Seriously.

The vampire comes back to life each evening, promptly at sundown a stirring as of bats begins. Like a convict to the chains, like the resolute gambler to her cards, like someone who's drunk wants wine (or whatever), the way *maggots gotta chew dead people.* The phantom rises, yawns, scrubs sleepy dirt and pleasant dreams from her gloomy tresses, flosses extended canines, disembarks. *Only a Treasury can make a vampire compleat.*

I want to fly away from the trappings of this coffin culture and rendezvous with C.A. Conrad on the astral plane. I buy *Mastering Astral Projection: 90-Day Guide to Out of Body Experience* by Robert Bruce and Brian Mercer. We'll walk around up there, tripping out on spiked Fiji water.

The truth of the flaneur: she browsed those banal structures at the beginning of a nightmare from which we are far from jolted. Before bed I consume chocolate, tobacco, alcohol, geese, the fat of geese, white poodle flesh wrapped round serrated plastic sheathed in batter and deep fried, and I eat ramps. Then I empty a quart into the milk jug and I lay supine and wait for sleep. If it doesn't come in a few minutes I crack the cotton on this bottle of pills and then it's like my torso suspends in lukewarm water until I'm talking with horses and fondling my siblings. *Beep beep.*

CHAPTER FIVE *THE TROUBLE*

I had diarrhea for four days before the Ariana Reines reading. The day of the reading I became desperate in anticipation of the captivity of performance and the potential for revelry afterwards. I was terribly embarrassed about the diarrhea to the extent that I didn't even want to say the word to Alli and instead referred to it as "the trouble." Even though Alli has had her mouth on every inch of my body. I kept thinking that even uttering the word "diarrhea" effected an intolerable withering of my sexiness.

After the fifth time I found myself emptying burning black water into the toilet at my office, I resolved to acquiesce to medication. I walked to the drug store and found they had a liquid medicine for diarrhea relief called Kaopectate and a generic medicine of the same formula called Walgreen's Diarrhea Relief. I was embarrassed enough to spend the extra three dollars for the Kaopectate which came disguised as cough syrup or a still potentially sexy herbal supplement.

Before the reading I was talking with Sarah and Cody, and Cody was talking about having recently seen an episode of *San Francisco Streets* in which they talk about the proliferation of "the bug," but what's "the bug?" Later they clarify it only to the extent that "the bug" is "v.d." but, we all wondered, *which kind?* Vampires are often associated with the plague, like ghosts whose deaths occurred before their life was finished. Dying before dying. But "the plague" too only occasionally obtains to specificity in the historical reconstruction of its wrath. As if specificity would improve communication between dimensions, as if the dead would start to *chew in their coffins* and upturn the earth.

After the reading I crawl back into my crypt, emulsify plasma and watch *Buffy*. And I don't have "the trouble." Even though one thing to say about Ariana's lush and icky writing is that my shame concerning "the trouble" is part of her theme, part of the semantics of the question she asked all of us: "are horrific acts necessary?" Did I have to spray hot liquid shit out of my ass for four days as a way of purging the summer? The heat of that filth a balm against the frigidity that spread over those months? What do you think?

The next day I decline to the café still flecked with crumbs of dirt and the flattened hair of the semi-dead. I order five bagels with extra cream cheese and while the barista gawks I eliminate three of them on the arduous seven foot charge from counter to door. The other two I play with like Renfield in the nuthouse, giving his pets names before concocting spider soufflé. I social network with these last two slathered chunks of carbs and say to myself, okay, huff this lactose, wait an hour and if there's not "the trouble" then go forth…

Meanwhile a song I haven't heard since I was a punk rat enters my head and I scour the wretched face of the Internet to find it. It's "Fuck the World" by The Queers. It sounds good as I'm considering outfit reality and covering these twin festering spots on the side of my neck with foundation. The fundamental premise is the refusal to work in deference to pursuing erotic pleasure ("I called in sick to work today / and laid in bed til noon") and performance of post-flanerie ("you and I will walk around / so pointlessly").

I go to Adobe Books and buy a copy of *Dracula* by Bram Stoker. And then sit at the café and reread *Action Kylie* by Kevin Killian. Kevin's writing gets me almost high with pleasure, and I walk to the theater to see the new Basquiat documentary with Lindsey and Steve. Beautiful youths parade around me, threatening to absorb me with their angles and outfits. Firemen on the corner of Valencia are loosening the hydrants and letting them spray onto the blacktop for a few seconds. Some of the youths jump in the foam and spray, and it reminds me of *Do The Right Thing* (1989, dir. Spike Lee), the fullest representation for my imagination of what "summer in New York" means. The ornaments of a summer *not arctic like this one.* When I walk by I look into the bitter eyes of the tanned, ripped firemen and reflect that while these hipsters douse themselves in cool water and make their sunglasses quiver with laughter, the firemen are at work.

At the end of the Basquiat documentary Julian Schnabel says "summer. … summer is a motherfucker in New York" while footage plays of young kids in the early 80s jumping in front of water billowing out a hydrant for their relief and for their pleasure in slow motion.

CHAPTER SIX *SLOOOWWWWW TRANSLATION*

I wanted to make my translation of *Le Vampire* by Charles Baudelaire so slow the mirror evacuates its reflection of the poem. But I could never tell whether I was the vampire or the one having her blood siphoned. So I could never tell who was enchanting who, but I can tell you that I more often than not came down on the side of shuddering in the mirror *if* anything was visible there. So the writing that spurts forth like ashes and foul spittle never knows from whence it comes or where it goes.

The dead move quick. But despite the tremendous acceleration of machinery, enabling modes of connection at unimaginable speeds, one of the first thing users did with the technology is slow the media. Slow it down so much that it aspires to total abstraction, in only grotesque relation to the original. The vampire is not a pure reflection of a regular count, mad for hoarding property. My wretched pale skin has no relation to the presumably beautiful time my parents had fucking.

The monstrous is always very slow. On the other hand, keep in mind that in the *Iliad* by Homer Achilles is described as pretty much the most fearsome man who walks the earth and yet far from being slow is impulsively *swift*. He can separate you from your esophagus while he's in bed with the slaves he daily rapes, chugging Orange Juliuses with his other hand. And then he'll wipe his mouth and drag your corpse around in the dirt in front of your parents and leave you out to gather mold until the blood beats red and strong into your capillaries and you rise, chest bared, a stake-sized niche as its ornament. On the other hand, if a turtle can beat this guy in a race, even once, what does that say for "the slow?" ?

Achilles recognized his slowness only in the land of the dead. In *Odyssey*, Odysseus, recognizing that all of his friends have become vampires, comes armed with buckets of blood. He spills them on the dark earth by his vessel on the threshold. Achilles says, "I would rather be a slave in the house of a pauper and be above ground than king of kings among the dead."

The dead are in the perfect tense. They mark the end of existence in the imperfect, fruition, flourishing. Perfection is precisely what Achilles wants to trade, and the price he'll pay in order to reattain imperfection is subsumption to slavery. He'll accept *negotium*, the structural lack of leisure, the theft of one's time by the propertied.

I guess it's a kind of talking-back to the Achilles of *Iliad* who had made the opposite of this very decision, to trade earthly endurance for the infinitely extended duration of glory. His oath then marks a recantation of glory-love in favor of a valorization of life even under the decrepitudinous yoke of obligatory work.

That's the same yoke whose call I answered all summer long. Slllloooowwwwly pulling myself out of this dream in which *Rodrigo* and *Roger* were one and the same, dressed in an ascot made *out of the perfumed flesh of puppies*. Wiping my disgusting white skin with a loofah and crawling into work, anxious and mellow. Anxiety like pure vampirism has no object. It performs its symptomatic allergy to the overproximity of the real and that's it. It was not always so easy to be me.

One of the possibilities for any piece of writing is the probability of its expiration. That it would find itself interred too deep or too fragile to ward off decay. Or be written in a language whose speakers all die or forget it. Although some abandoned languages die without dying. Plato's Greek. Baudelaire's French. For these texts which are abandoned without expiring, translation is how they find resuscitation. Benjamin describes translation as just this wizardry: bringing about the *afterlife* of a text.

In the Platono-Socratic critique of writing, writing goes into the world, and the effects of its circulation cannot be predicted, reckoned, known, not ever, as long as there remains the potential for any kind of reading or rending into something. *Even a thing which moves so slow it's terrifying.* Nobody is scared of a turtle although all of my friends would flinch at turtle stew. Their bleeding heads would screw into a grimace and look up like, you expect me to feast on this?

CHAPTER SEVEN *THE WIG*

All my writing adheres to rhythm, starving for clotted plasma, for plethoric erotic productivity. Writing under siege. Writing in the wens and lesions of the vampire's body, in the daylight when the administration would be too bright to see. In time past we called the lesion the field, culled root vegetables out of it and made soup. Before the ontogenesis of the categorically undead scrawling their names on deeds.

The emergence of vampires in Europe is concomitant with the formation of parliaments, the drawing of borders in black forests, the institutionalization of the Romanian language. The first thief and the first policeman chasing the thief. Dazzling badges. Some half-bat running off into headphones shouting fuck the partitioners of the sensible. Coming straight out the underground. How *Buffy* would it be to crack this stalk and restage that originary curse over a shared box of saturated fat and jelly. *I saw a dummy. It gave me the wig.*

In *Buffy the Vampire Slayer,* there are two kinds of vampires. There are the very recently dead who haplessly crawl out of the earth, so starved for blood they're senseless. These are the ones who find, instead of dinner, Buffy waiting for them, Mr. Pointy in her hand, ready to whip upon their ass for 60-90 seconds before plunging the stake into their chest and turning them into screaming, dissolving ash. After witnessing almost identical scenes dozens of times, one might wonder why these vamps don't wise up, perhaps emerge from the grave more flexible about performing their vocation and more attentive to negotiating a way of surviving slayage. But it's the sole desire driving their will. This hunger appearing as if from an invisible interior commanding them to go and eat.

The other genus, however, eschews the immediate search for errant teenagers in favor of alternate activities. Often under the umbrage of some visiting demon or union head, these while away *the working night* in discussion, playful combat, or even drink. And yet the conventional notions of the vampire indicate no surplus time for such pursuits. Just as the vampire bat must consume 50-100% of its own body weight in blood each night, once someone has become a vampire, that's their sole vocation. The sun going down is the whistle calling them to work, the su's reappearance heralds their fiery quittin' time. How are we to understand this apparent dissimulation?

This latter group of bloodsuckers is also distinguished from the former by the fact that apparently by an act of will they can by affecting a placid interior demeanor effect a human face, free from the migraine-scar pose of the vampire. This allows them to walk the earth, at night of course, as if they were just any human. Essentially vampiric, these demons wear the wig.

Michel de Certeau describes *la perruque,* or "the wig," as a diversionary practice, as an art. "La perruque is the worker's own work disguised as work for his (sic) employer." It's not pilfering, because nothing "of material value" is stolen and not absenteeism in that the worker is "there."

De Certeau's examples are writing a love letter on company time or "borrowing" equipment to make one's own piece of furniture. "In the very place where the machine he must serve reigns supreme, he cunningly takes pleasure in finding a way to create gratuitous pro-ducts whose sole purpose is to signify his own capabilities through his work and to confirm his solidarity with other workers or his family." *I too have a duty to do, a duty to others, a duty to you, a duty to the dead.*

Poor vampires to have to be the recurrent gothic metaphor Marx uses to describe the capitalist. Caught between categorical worlds and forced to sell their disposable time. The emergence of vampires is concomitant with their appropriation of the night time as a space in which to maintain constant production and the development of the shift system. You know how it's extremely deleterious to work at night, harmful to the body to never wallow in the light of the sun? Pity the vampire, then, whose allergy to light forces her to work in unnatural hours. Although work as we know it is unnatural. Maybe later we can talk about work being natural or unnatural, but only after the omnipresent condition of exploitation based on an originary cleft between those who own and those who do not is overturned. Until then, pity the vampire. All of us.

That cleft mirrors the twin traditions of vampires. After Stoker most of our culture refers to what we can term the "Dracula" tradition of vampires. The Dracula tradition privileges the aristocratic and militaristically heroic condition of the vampire. The historic figure Stoker bases Dracula on, after all, finds its first literary citation in the English translation of *Capital.* The boyar siphoning surplus value out of what he rents. All of his powers of enchantment and seduction, the ability to shift shapes and buy land must be read in terms of his power to exploit those who only have their own bodies to sell. Finally, that's all he's interested in, the goo that squirts through their hearts and animates torsos at the lathe. I have *always* wanted to write a text in which I reference the lathe, and I am overjoyed at the occasion of this translation to do so.

Meanwhile, another kind of vampire exists, predating the historically-inflected figure of the Count. These are beasts, always understood to exist on the threshold between the animal and the human. The lupine motifs that saturate later Dracula myths likely originate in the local symbology of these earlier monsters, who are literally part wolf and part man. Until they, you know, *buy land.* This vampire, just as the innumerable mad *famished* dissolve under the impress of the slayer's stake, disappears from the cultural record as is typical of the subjugated and landless. They return, to some extent, in more contemporary representations, like *Buffy,* but forever under the insignia of the doomed, the expiring, the dispossessed, the rotting mite in the dustbin of history.

Poor vampires. Poor *me.* I do feel bad about overtaking carbohydrates in reckless abundance, about drinking the blood from necks, about my irrational hatred for my neighbor's dog who like me only wants his body groomed by touch; about loving Leslie inadequately. I feel guilty towards the object of my future self at the moment of my death, counting the innumerable hours I was forced to sell in order to keep charmed chum flailing from buckets to inside me.

That anticipatory guilt with no object drives both Angel and Spike to attempt suicide on *Buffy.* Angel, convinced that his staying in Sunnydale will bring about Buffy's death, crests a high hill and waits for sunlight. Part of the work of light is to shrivel the skin of vampires and reduce them to ash. Spike builds a machine with a long, thick stake which he attempts to land on chest-first. He fails. He gets up, panting, disappointed.

Le Vampire by Charles Baudelaire is in part a prayer to objects. *Kill me,* the poem says to a dagger. *Kill me,* the poem says to a flagon of poison. He describes death as a freedom, a freedom from ennui and the emerging regime of work and subjection coming to own the world all around him. The objects are clear in their refusal. The poet doesn't deserve that freedom. After all, the dagger and the poison know that all Baudelaire really wants is to forego the abjection of impoverishment and the obligation to work in order to pursue erotic pleasure. Scraping fingers grooming the tiny bee-fur draping his balls and asshole. Wash of the tongue. Flowering mall.

CHAPTER EIGHT
I WAS A TEENAGE OR LIKE TWENTY TWO YEAR OLD VAMPIRE

Lisa and I have seen each other 3 times this summer after not speaking for 7 years. We had been very close friends, wrenched and tortured in the way of people who make an erotic compact based on the premise that they would never fuck despite mutual and diffuse libidinal longings. And then stopped being friends, hence the 7 years of silence, but did so without any legible crisis or reciprocal disdain, at least any I was aware of.

She's saying Jennifer had a baby. We're sitting on a bench in the dog park in Cole Valley in the middle of August, it's *freezing*, and we're smoking cigarettes and watching outbound and inbound N Judah trains rumble in and out of the tunnel. Our sociability this evening has been steady and pleasant; she's just married and moving to New York City in a week and I notice that we are right now enacting a play which has the potential force of two characters who will *never see each other again*. We get along with utmost familiarity but there's none of that erotic spark which brought us together as youths.

Our first meeting had been the opportunity for the full procedural catch-up, as we each recited a litany of our once-mutual acquaintances and descriptions of their stations in life. I told her about Steve and Matthew and Jennifer. She told me about, oh, whoever, I can't remember their names. I remember her one friend who was a native San Franciscan and although in her mid-20s and living with roommates returned to her parent's house once a day to shit.

Still, *that* was the tacitly determined space for such indexing. Thus very *not* apropos for Lisa to be talking about Melissa's new baby in this dog park, seeing as we're about fifteen minutes from this slightly charged moment of maybe *never seeing each other again*. Aren't we supposed to perhaps revisit, even if only as an object of contemplation, our former erotic charge before its dissipation? Why would I want to hear about Melissa's baby or Melissa at all? I read it as something like punishment, but perhaps that's too strong a word. Perhaps instead Lisa intuited somehow that I was in the process of freezing the translation of Charles Baudelaire's poem "Le Vampire" and she recalled this vampiric turn I had taken in my early 20s.

The main problem with me dating Melissa was that I sort of hated her and wasn't attracted to her at all. So imagine how much I resented myself for spending all this time courting her. For the two weeks we dated I spent every moment plotting how to make Jennifer love me again and resurrect me from the dead. I was staying with Jennifer in our apartment and sleeping with Melissa in her railroad flat on Fell Street. Sleeping with her but not fucking her. I wanted to suck her blood, but giving her a taste of my own bound me to her in some meaningful way I couldn't stand.

One night at a party at which Melissa and Jennifer both attended I drank ten bottles of wine and pulled Jennifer onto the stoop for a frank discussion of did she love me again, would she bring me back to life. Did she understand that I was dead without having died and that I was overwhelmed by an urge to spread this condition to innocent young women all over San Francisco. Did she ever consider that perhaps the indecision she felt regarding her desires was, in practice, bad feminism? Melissa overheard the whole thing and made a huge display of storming past the two of us on the stoop, her face twisted into a grimace, and pouting off into the night. God I hated her. But that didn't stop me from calling her later that night over and over until finally she answered, taking a cab with money I did not have to her flat on Fell Street, finally submitting to her hand wrenching my cock until it was if not hard at least *rigor mortis* and pushing it inside her.

I know how this sounds. It makes me cringe too. It's like I'm in that weird little broom closet on *The Real World* where they make the housemates confess their inner feelings. And I know this portrait of myself as a wrathful, pathetic, brutal jerk is ugly. Welcome to the world of Charles Baudelaire.

Melissa refused to be in the same room with me after, which is what really aggravated Lisa. Lisa finally only wanted a placid social triangulation between her two closest friends, Melissa and Brandon, and now she had to face a maelstrom. The riverbank hated Achilles for a while too, you know. Dialectics hates catastrophe, its very own Dante's *Inferno*.

Anyway, Melissa's revenge on me for turning her into the undead was not becoming a rich doctor and having a baby. Her revenge on me manifests every time I ring somebody's doorbell. It is well known that the threshold is a fraught space for vampires. One evening during our fortnight of operatic ambivalence Melissa came to my house and rang the doorbell. There was no buzzer to open the door, so I had to walk down a long flight of stairs to open the door for visitors. The whole way down the stairs I could see her on the front porch, her entire body visible in the glass pane that held the door together in the middle. She looked up the stairs expectantly, watching me watching her, unconsciously biting her lower lip and wistfully regarding her beloved descending a staircase. As I apprehended this scene I reflected on my hatred for her, for myself, for the long life of the undead ahead. And to this day when I ring someone's doorbell and a pane of glass holds the door together, I move out of the way, or turn my back to it. I don't want to be the object of their optical loathing, which I project like a sharpened stake.

CHAPTER NINE
A HEMISPHERE IN JUSTIN BIEBER'S HAIR

One tremendous lesson of Nietzsche's work and *Buffy The Vampire Slayer* is that trouble always arrives with the attempt to change what you are. I'm not the first or the only one to lean onto material and lick my lips in anticipation of whatever vital resided inside it. I'm not the first one to beg one's mother. I was not given the genetically impeccable gift of poetry whispered into my ear crisp as a basket of snakes. I was not given the genetically impeccable hair of Justin Bieber.

O Justin, let me breathe in for a long time, for a long long long long time, the odor of your hair. Let me plunge my face into it like *a drinker to the jug of wine,* and let me agitate you with my moustache. Let me leave you a souvenir of this hair thing. If you could know all that I see! All the things I feel! All that I intend to do in your hair. My body will take a vacation upon that scent like a thoughtful trip to Hawaii. Your scalp is like a couch and I'm lying on it. Your scalp is like a yacht, rocked by the rolling waves, rocking in between jugs full of blood and flowers full of blood. I mess up my mouth and smoke cigarettes afterwards. I'm drunk without drinking; I'm drunk on the stench of it. Elastic headbands in your hair. *I want to munch your memoirs!*

CHAPTER TEN *MEMORIAL DAY*

In the aquarium at Coney Island we watched a trained sea otter perform with his trainer. Startling flips and displays, bad absorption of the *logos,* facts and figures concerning its species. At one point, the otter used one of its wide, webbed back feet to mimic the dorsal fin of the Great White Shark while the hunk on the microphone informed us glibly that the sea otter was preyed upon by sharks in the wild and the *Jaws* theme croaked out of the p.a. so obvious but it still got some laughs. Masquerading as the thing which hunts it. Compelled to do so in order to earn the day's bucket of scented chum.

Dana made a joke later about a film concerning human life, starring a melanoma. But in fact art that dramatizes our precarity among predators proliferates. There are animals and intra-special hunters. And then that other, special species…on the threshold of life and death…of animal and human…the carnophallogocentric entity which is yet not quite reasonable: Iraqis, I mean vampires. *At the worst it can only be death. And a man's death is not a calf's.*

Before or after the demonstration of his own predators I can't remember, the sea otter smacks his trainer on the ass seductively. It's flirty in only the most robotic way but still WTF? I saw sea horses eating each other. Two of us saw somebody walking into the aquarium with a bag full of goldfish. Blood for Dracula. Blood for the deranged carnivorous sea horses whose molars sizzle at the thought of animated goldfish. Deranged barons with a taste for the blood that squirts out of one's finger. Be careful with that bread. The tenacious abjection of life in the tank. Gooey booger-capped kids' paws blocking one's already compromised view.

When Alli texted me "Sorry to have to send some sad news – Leslie died last night" I was on the F train going to Coney Island. Dana and I were standing in a car by ourselves, waiting for the crowds to dissipate somewhat so we could jump to the car behind us where we hoped we'd find our friends. We waited together for *what felt like an eternity* in the subway station on 1st and Houston, the very station in which he and I had waited for a train the year before for a memorably long time. The eventual return of the merely annoying, like how vampires in Slovakia are often derived from real life dickheads. This year, like last year, it was just-bearably hot. We all went from pleasant to grouch. The wait was a reminder of all things that test one's patience: late-arriving trains, ambient, user-manipulated translations of Justin Bieber's work, poetry. The neurosomatic experience of the painfully tardy and nefariously ponderous. The curse of everlasting life.

The train comes, although it's so stuffed we have to squeeze in separate cars.

Somewhere mid-Brooklyn we finally changed cars. Instead of telling the group that Alli texted me to say that Leslie died last night, Dana told them and indicated that this news had arrived through my phone. I stood there like an embarrassed messenger, ashamed to be holding onto this meme in its particular encryptions. I had the feeling that I shouldn't be the one—that this wasn't my message, the declarative fact of Leslie's death. Speech I didn't understand thoroughly enough to claim, like a surprising hunger for human blood I don't want to *sate but I've just got to. Chomp chomp chomp.*

After we got back from Coney Island we hung out with Julian at xis apartment in Brooklyn. We sat and drank tequila and read pages of Leslie's work together and then when it was time to change the record Julian told me I could put something on and I put on Too Short's classic *Life Is Too Short.*

CHAPTER ELEVEN *CUSSWORDS*

As a kid I had a copy of *Life Is Too Short* on a cassette tape that I shoplifted from the mall. The music store at the mall is where I stole all the tapes that would turn me into a poet. Before I made a practice of stealing time every day from my employers I was in the habit of shoplifting from retail outlets: cigarettes, candy, cassette tapes.

At least twice a day I rode my bicycle from my house to Casey's, a sort of gas station and what I call now in my adult life a "corner store" although the quasi-rural ecology of my hometown did not really permit of "corners" per se. I rode my bike to Casey's to buy soda, because before I was addicted to alcohol I was addicted to high fructose corn syrup as a vehicle for caffeine. Later I shoplifted cigarettes and candy from Casey's too. For some reason the owner of Casey's also built small storage units for rent in the back parking lot and that's where you would go to get your ass kicked or kick someone's ass in junior high school. And smoke cigarettes. Before I was addicted to cigarettes I shoplifted them and smoked them breezily at Casey's.

I had a portable cassette player and often times on my bike ride I'd play *Life Is Too Short.* Actually, I think I just listened to one song over and over again: "Cusswords."

"Cusswords" is an eight minute long song with no chorus that defers its central thematic until the very end. That is, while the lyrics of "Cusswords" are indeed laden with cusswords, the assertion that cusswords have a kind of talismanic power (specifically, to ease the burden of the prisoner in lockdown, but perhaps to be read as an allegory for liberation in a general sense) is not uttered until the final seconds of the jam. This deferral is one way in which "Cusswords" eschews the verse/chorus dialectic. Instead it's performative catastrophe, synced to the entropy of the afterlife.

"What is life? / Life is too short…" Paging Dracula, right? Life is too short, compared to death obviously. But there's another proposition as to the meaning of life. "If you ask me what it's all about / I'll say it's about that money." This observation precedes one of the most famous moments of Too Short's career: the fantasy scene in which Ronald Reagan approaches him to ask his advice about the U.S. economy and the state of cancer research; Too

Short responds by expressing shock that Reagan could live in the White House without actively dealing cocaine, and boasts that recently Nancy Reagan herself had visited Too Short in Oakland to give him fellatio. Corn on the cob is proposed. Not disregarding the terrifying particulars of this astonishing sequence, it's worth nothing: Too Short's association of money and time in the jam. The brevity of time and the scarcity of money. And then there's us, reading Leslie's poems with "Cusswords" as our soundtrack, laughing and wincing over mismatched glasses of fermented plasma.

CHAPTER TWELVE *ANOTHER MEMORIAL DAY*

The religious parts of the ceremony were moving and uncanny to me, who shares the vampire's traditional distaste for anything transcendentally beautiful. The rituals that refrain in my life pretend to be allergic to smoldering incense and rhythmic bells, and all of the awkwardness of my body traversing the monastic site recalled the sublime awkwardness which was Leslie's sociability.

The other unique thing for me was the apotheosis of Leslie Scalapino, the poet. Those who spoke recited her own lines to the urn of ashes on the altar. Her work was heaving in the room as if to guarantee its inextinguishability. Leslie's body had been translated into ash and filed into an urn. The body of her work walks the earth and occupies the rhythmic force of many bodies. Her prosodies structured the molecules of the air. Like that.

Wine and snacks after the ceremony. We heard that it had already been hard to convince the monastery to permit the serving of meat much less alcohol. Lamb in a cilantro sauce, hummus and chips, lots of cheese, Chardonnay and Zinfandel from Leslie and Tom's cellar. Little cups of that ethereal fire, éclair-shaped, rose out of limpid space.

After the memorial service for Leslie the poets went to a bar called the Pelican. The Pelican looks outside and in like a real English pub, something like perhaps the one Jon Bon Jovi had constructed on his estate in New Jersey and at which he drinks beer with Bruce Springsteen. Not just in my fantasies, but in real life. I went out to smoke and my eye caught light —dazzling off of silver, gaudy streamers inexplicably lining the pub's roof.

Like raking the dirt packing you into the box and realizing *I'm dead* one peers out at one's community and asks *how*? A drug-addicted farm boy with questionable aptitude for reading comprehension and social grace, wielding rather oversize incisors. Huck Finn with a library card and a peculiar taste for *very very very rare meat.* Yet simply and with almost no reflection, I befriended my heroes and didn't have to travel to the land of the dead to do it. This is the pop mischief through which my political existence obtains. This is how my machinery processes thought. Of Leslie, of all rhythms, of all spectacle. Dazzling plastic lining the pub as if its skin were made of shimmering cilantro.

CHAPTER THIRTEEN *THE NIGHTMARE*

I wake from this nightmare, panting, hearing the echo of the terrified screams my own diaphragm contrived to slit the silence of the night. In the nightmare, I motivate trained tigers in a board room. Sloshing in through the windows come sea otters gone awry, gone rogue, gone land/board room. I've picked, one by one, the fascist hairs that pout out my face. I've taken in a train with killer whales in bloated khakis. Ripping the perfumed flesh of children and steaming a crepe for Charles Baudelaire who loved to smell the flesh of children just before he ate.

I wake from this nightmare, panting, hearing the echo of the terrified screams my own diaphragm contrived to slit the silence of the night. In the nightmare, the mall came to the rats. And bees were there, reading beelets with their mouth in the shrubs of the mall, in the foliage crowding in the perimeters of my sociability. And we found puppies there, and cyborg otters, expert in the epistolary novel, the supreme genre of rats. So I imposed my libidinal anvil onto all of them in advance. Rosaries and switchblades. Everything can happen in this mall just as in the antiquated one except I can't feel your fur quiver in my teeth.

I wake from this nightmare, panting, hearing the echo of the terrified screams my own diaphragm contrived to slit the silence of the night. In the nightmare, the economy of the sign still prevailed. Utterances appeared and they were not goblinesque. In fact they conformed to the comportment of fricatives and effervescent vowel movement. I said the mall is in full flower and everybody gets it. We stand around congratulating each other, having finally found a syntax for expressing the sexual desires we harbor for parents, aunts and uncles. Having forgotten the death of this economy, I welcomed it to join our party, slurping oysters in the penumbral patio and frying in the sun.

I wake from this nightmare, panting, hearing the echo of the terrified screams my own diaphragm contrived to slit the silence of the night. In the nightmare, I dictate my autobiography to Christian Slater in a hotel room above Market Street. I lie about the quantity of beverages and bagels and pregnant quarts of pharmaceutical opiates that droop over with the pearline gaze of a junkie. Children of the night. The autobiography sells like crazy and yet Christian Slater squats on my chest in Florida. *Mon frère,* I try and

gasp it at him, get him to stop feeling so free with his excremental needs.
Mon frère! Hypocrite lecteur! My pants constrict my neck like a handkerchief
drawn too tight.

I wake from this nightmare, panting, hearing the echo of the terrified
screams my own diaphragm contrived to slit the silence of the night. In the
nightmare, I go into the underworld to hear the tales the dead speak. Also to
retrieve my beloved Justin Beiber, dead before his time. He's got an angelic
voice *but I'm Orpheus motherfuckers* and this is clear because when I open my
mouth you can see all manner of little dogs run up to me with their tongues
swinging low like the chain of Jibbs. In Hell you have to speak Ancient
Greek and I do it beautifully. I pour slimy ounces of the black blood into the
dark earth and then I see him. There's only one prematurely dead wraith
with hair that beautiful in all of Hell. That's my man. Moments later, as his
tiny knees dig into the space between my ribs and cut off the flow of carbon
monoxide out of my lips, I realize he's not Beibs at all, but a beastly
incarnation of Charles Baudelaire. He's got Justin Bieber's hair but that old
assy ascot.

I wake from this nightmare, panting, hearing the echo of the terrified
screams my own diaphragm contrived to slit the silence of the night. In the
nightmare, I'm reading my favorite poem, "Le Vampire." Only I can't finish
it. The reading takes days, takes weeks, takes over my day job, interferes
with my desires for sociability which are essentially *to suck the blood out of as
many people as possible.* To turn as many as I can into mirror images of myself.
How easy would projection be then? How Charles Baudelaire would it be if
I started talking about *the unseemly jade* with whom I practice *simple sucking?*
But it's still just me, gumming my own wounds, pricking tears in my flesh
with a stinger like a deranged bee.

I wake from this nightmare, panting, hearing the echo of the terrified screams
my own diaphragm contrived to slit the silence of the night. In the nightmare,
I break down into the molecules of my own chatter. Before Spike was Spike
he was William the Bloody and before he was William the Bloody he was a
mediocre Victorian poet whose prosody had a very explicit intended effect: to
draw love towards his body. Along with the only possession I have to sell,
that is, my presence in the stable of the men who own me, all I've got is love
and guilt. It's ugly and deformed. It's bloated and it leaks a besmirched fluid.
A gunk that smells of dimes. The body of a vampire.

CORRESPONDENCES

CORRESPONDENCES

Something I meant to do…something *unnatural.*
Squeeze a pill between my tonsils. See what the
tonsure does to my temples? Makes my brain look bigger?
I see you looking at me—familiar and observant.

There's a noise that saturates Oakland. I'm confident
it saturates the helium deposits pilloried
in the nitrate-rich boneyard of the bay.
I know! That sound stirred me too

from the orgiastic perfume of a delightful dream
in which I munched the profundity of not one,
not two…but like *five* children,
their lives and their flaky attention

cool as the skin of leftover plums.
Sorry to make Charles Baudelaire a cannibal.
It was hard enough to be him. Sorry
to suggest this gastrophagous bent consumed
him and that remarkable ascot.

Oh fine, be incensed. For a minute, on the train, I saw
you loving its sound. Its spirit. Its essence.

CORRESPONDENCES

I don't think language is light
but something sees through the floating corset
passing through the colon of this salsa
I chug it with my familiars.
Nothing really resembles anything else
and language is not light.
Hold up this page, you're just trying to
conjugate plastic.
It doesn't. There are sovereigns so fabulous

they delight in roasting children.
A horrible Baudelaireanism to include
in this translation for you
who have just painted a nursery. Did you all
decide on taupe or emerald? Nevermind
they do not delight in roasting children
but rather tomatillos. The whining skins
of peppers. Corn. Corn from
musky, incendiary tubes.

CORRESPONDENCES

Omigod the *natural* spare
me. Elaborate routinization of genetic entropy
so guys passing by give me those salty looks
(Lawry's) The seats of Ferraris feel familiar,

like the caress of a sibling in prehistory.
Fossilized moss fondues,
dense as old cake, profound as Modernism;
vast crumb fondue which I duly, you know, buy online.

Perfume is colorless, my dudes,
just like my siblings. We're hot, we're related,
we emerge in the prairies like a twist
on the chalupa. Wet the wrapper if you want

it to stick. If you want to be rich,
if you want to be triumphant. Make it clap
the pods of you, but don't start lecturing
me about "the natural."

I just told a barista that I have
a twin brother. And yet I wasn't
even so much "born" as set-down-
adjacent-to-these-other-things.

CORRESPONDENCES

Things do not connect, they correspond. Except
when they do not correspond, and then sometimes
you find yourself "mowing the yard." Nobody
knows how swiftly the cannibal inside these lines

rears, wags the salt shaker at thighs striding by. Glorious
tights simply the shrink-wrap on what cats
simply have to plow. Ever since Charles Baudelaire
initiated modernity, cracking nuts between his teeth

and *shrieking* that the nuts were like the heads
of little children in his mouth. *Eeek*! But
did you eat it? Or did you have a *correspondence*
with it? Did it wriggle inside the paper bag,

nipping at your fingers? Bummer. Syphilis is a bummer.
Slave labor is a bummer. And there's us, unwashed and
modern, sipping Maalox on an airplane.

CORRESPONDENCES

Somehow I've got to tempt life into pill shape.
There's confidence so confident it would irradiate
Aderol withdrawal. In the rich, mealy, Burgundian
shadow of an ass that has never known paper,
look at me now. Look at me freak clearly,
freak clarity. Freak correspondence. In high-
chairs there sit babes, slimy with virus,
gnawing on pork tenderloin with their brittle,
mortal, valuable teeth. They're fed by the
pill-flecked hands of prairie baby daddies.

Hillbilly heroin. It makes life a work
of extravagant pharmacircuitry. Hillbilly...*correspondence*.
Desperate to surpass the back Ozark
crank freak inside me, desperate not to
blow what I only ever intended to cook.
This used to be my walk now it's my ambience.
It makes dinner out of what should be insulating
the shack our babies chow in. Those
drug-addled spider-loving swine,
greedier than ever for crystal focus.

CORRESPONDENCES

I put my head in mud and it is cool.
I mean my scalp tingles with the yesterday's-gravy-
chill of the improbably frigid. Like dandruff
shampoo, only nasty and made out of worms.
And the pee of young loutish boys making ornery
at the wedding as it tumbles into legend.
Also the mud, my putting my head into it,
makes me *awesome*. Industry is the enemy
of magic—all the more reason to do it
on a divan made of newt's eyes (or whatever.)
To *do the nasty* on a davenport woven of
sage tendrils and grunt in Coptic.

Two hot boys approach, their veins green
as the forests of Egypt. You know, where holy ones
chant together *in Coptic*. I corrupt
them with money and industry. I choose
them over infinity, their musk over my
musk. I magically choose these boys,
and we sit to eat together at a banquet
laden with cutlery. Laden with mud pies.

CORRESPONDENCES

I was standing between two pillars when, oh
shit! they started talking to me. What
passes as a party in the forest of the
totally symbolic? What passes as a fond

party in one's loins in the totally unpartylike
profundity of brutal partying? I don't
know whether it's the Visine™ or Everyday Life™
but I swear I heard pillars whispering to me.

They said, "Hey, Charles Baudelaire,
everything is in correspondence, but also
you're leaking all over an oboe. Kill children.
Write a poem." This is how I begin to balloon.

This is how my tinkle gets tickled. I go
to this party and my pupils dissolve into
a saline typhoon that trolls absorb into
their saliva. Recapitulated piñata interior.

Major party. It's *my* party. And I will
cum on an oboe if I…um…need to?

CORRESPONDENCES

La la la

I sing into the air which today
feels gray as an abandoned condom
brimming with yesterday's semen...
isn't that image so Charles Baudelaire?

Really, everything feels fine, familiar:
the longing that confounds my lines
just the tenebrous, profound unity
of a given workday under given conditions.
In the new Taylor Swift song she
crashes a wedding and steals the groom. It's not
her best work, perhaps, but still a sort
of *triumph of the other!*

And the brazen expansion of her *genius*
a pabulum I will gnaw as musk,
as unenlivened odor. I'm not going
to eat kids. And yet I am going
to. On a fucking magic carpet!

CORRESPONDENCES

I'm not going to shear a sheep and eat
wool for lunch. That is *so* uncool.
Instead, I buck tin and sip on the swarming
content of my closest friends.

As soon as one of us bails out this burning
clipper ship we'll flail in correspondence.
Donnie from NKOTB, as if from the air,
calls out to me, the best translator ever of
Charles Baudelaire. Whose ascot
hangs tough. Whose coiffure hangs tough.

My clippers puff. But you already know. You
shaved last night's bleating horde.
And then we drank the distilled liquor
that cradled a rotting shark's head. In the future.
In the curdled rehearsal of the modern.

CORRESPONDENCES

At Starbucks they're showing a portrait of one
of their slaves lugging a big basket of beans
on his shoulder. They're really rubbing "it"
in my face and / or I'm really rubbing "it"
in my own face. Heinous laziness that pricks
one's visage. Source and mouth of a
BLOOD RIVER pooling in one's septum,
spewing into futurity. I came here to write in my, um,
dream journal. A coup of nastiness gathers as a sourness
on our tongues in unison, crewing us who only
meant to accrue stimulation among babes. My dreams
are full of oboes, moms, perfumes. Musky like the treasured
smell of yesterday's fuck still murmuring on the
lip. Immiseration of the criminal proletariat
plays as scalding water pulverizing fruit.

I was heinous and lazy. I did it for babes.
But I did it for historic babes.

CORRESPONDENCES

Little pricks in the phlegmatic dome through which
passes the confused speech I parade unleashed
into the travesty known as my fellows
and sisters, each singing with their domes
forming little pricks that warm on us familiar.
I feel a little bit like I was born, then we
met, and since then I'm writing to you in *correspondence,*
inarticulate…tenebrous…profound as a stale
Neapolitan cracker/cookie hybrid from like the
Stockholm airport, which is to say:
the pleasure of certain smells, little pricks.
The salinity of the sucked oyster and how
loop-ass it makes one, hovering over the
Pont Royal to this of all possible triumphs.
Little barbs of pricks against the total administration
and surveillance of this flight-arresting
pansomatic musky orgasm. Don't be insensitive,
my song. Tell Rob *hi* and *thanks.*
Be the little prick of which you sing.
Deplane. Follow the sign that reads CORRESPONDANCES.

PARIS DREAM

The stars in Baudelaire represent a picture puzzle of the commodity. They are the ever-same in great masses.
—Walter Benjamin

A last, general rule: in love, beware of the moon and the stars; beware of the Venus de Milo.   —Charles Baudelaire

Excuse me for feeling this moment is critical. —Paris Hilton

I live in a lousy place for stars. But that doesn't mean that I don't like stars. I was shocked when I told Alli that I was translating the poem *Paris Dream* by Charles Baudelaire in part by thinking about how the stars twinkle in his work and she said, "But you hate the stars." What was her evidence? I was stumped. Who *hates stars?* I proposed that she was conflating my admitted distaste for dogs and other animals with a general displeasure for…what? I mean I could see perhaps reading someone's dislike for dogs as a dislike for, say, other non-human mammals or even certain kinds of flora and fauna. But, and I ask again: who *hates the stars*?

You don't often see the stars in San Francisco because an advection, characterized by the lateral transfer of temperature by wind blowing over cooler water, generates fog. The fog comes when warm, moist air blows from the central Pacific Ocean across the cold water of the California Current, which flows just off the coast. Baudelaire loved the fog. The spatial abyss of solitude finding consolation in a shroud…you know…*the masses.*

Running late to my pastoral Latin poetry reading group, I stopped on Valencia by the haute coffee shop because I saw Michael Cera and Charlyne Yi huddled together, smiling so sweetly over the white cups—cups any non-haloed slob able to spend $4.50 on a shot of espresso can also use. I walked by, thought "that was Michael Cera and Charlyne Yi," and even though I was late I had to stop, drawn back through the fog from which I was emerging like a comet (a star with hair) and retrace my steps, this time with one medium-long lingering gaze at Cera, whose celebrated charisma was all-too-familiar amidst the warm furniture of the coffee shop. I love their coffee, it's fruity and never scalds. Like Cera's affect, which I treasure. I want to know the future of Michael Cera's career as an actor. Like how's his middleperiod. I ask the stars—but they're just as quiet as the fog.

If I'm desperate to try and see the stars, I've got to first make it to the window through the hoard of stranded commodities in my room. I've got to navigate piles of books, kick over stale eclairs, overturn the natural. Sweltering against the sides of a blunt machete I no longer even know how to wield, I never knew how to wield a machete although now I can recognize the flight of syllables as they spread through Europe. Or I like how Lisa Robertson writes it, "the hotel of Europe."

I look out—but all I can see is the sex my neighbors are having, frozen in the distance like they're a painting of their own sex. As much as I might be enjoying this, I am certain they'd enjoy it more and I wish I could share it with them. But, then again, do you want to see a painting of yourself fucking?

You know how Baudelaire sometimes wants to be a glittering hero and sometimes wants to inhabit a world in which there's no light ever anymore? There was never anything hot about watching the neighbors—perhaps because the distance makes their movements occur as if they were fucking in stone, like the vision of motion in the poem of Parmenides. That was a pretty chaste reference, *mais non?*

In 2004, I really wanted to try and watch *1 Night In Paris,* or at least to try and see what it looked like. The stills that accompanied articles about its release made it seem like a painting: the scene seemed so green, filthy, the Rembrandt-light of surveillance footage. Not real sex with real bodies, but colliding glass and Black American Express cards. I couldn't find it. Lost in the labyrinth of celebrity porn sites and ads popping out of the labyrinth's walls like abyssal riddles, themselves labyrinthine, I got lost. I gave up. Once I had enough resolve to walk up to the porn store by my house whose marquee had read *Spend 1 Night In Paris* all Autumn, and then amended for the holiday season to read *The Perfect XXXmas: 1 Night In Paris.* I walked to the door but just ended up pacing out front.

Nick Ut's *Paris Hilton is seen through the window of a police car as she is transported from her home to court by the Los Angeles County Sheriff's Department in Los Angeles on Friday June 8, 2007* is part of the magnificent *Exposed* show on the third floor of the SFMOMA. In the next room there's another photo by Ut, the famous picture of Phan Thị Kim Phúc running naked and screaming from a napalm attack in Vietnam. The pictures as it happen are taken on the same exact day, 35 years apart.

Ut's picture of Hilton going to jail is, by all including his account, a failure. It's the photographer standing next to Ut, Karl Larsen, who takes the finally canonical shot of Hilton's tears. It's Larsen's that will light up the perfunctory Google image search. Ut's picture, in stark contrast to the overcast horror in the photo of 1972, almost appears as if it were taken in the same room in which *One Night In Paris* goes down. Only in daylight. You can't see the stars in daylight, but, you know, they are there.

Ut's photo is cut more or less in half, diagonally, with a reflection of something, perhaps a camera strap. It looks like a reflection of thick electric wires, making a scar where Hilton's forehead meets her hair, performing a kind of adumbrated lobotomy. There's something gorgeous about how whatever it is divides the picture into two since the experience of seeing it generates a stream of doubles. The spectator and the commodified object (the photo), the photographer and his subject, the inside and outside of the cop car and ultimately the tears of Phan Thi Kim Phúc against the tears of the heiress.

There are two men in the background, not cops. Both I think are wearing white t-shirts, though the fuzzy reds at the top of the picture infiltrate the figure on the left. He's wearing a jacket—it's June in L.A. Was it chilly. You can't see their faces, but their bodies look ambivalent, tired, already over the drama of the scene. And in that way they echo exactly the soldiers lining the road down which Phan Thi Kim Phúc runs.

All those reds—the reflection of flash bulbs in the car window? They are exactly the color of Paris's face: smudgy and ethereal. Indeed, the regular crispness of her image as it emerges in the paparazzial canon now seems ghostly—dead before her death. You can't see but infer her tears. Her mouth is open, eyes closed. Mid-sob. The photograph freezes the sob into total expectancy, and thus prolongs it eternally. The very left part of her face is cropped, the vertical line bisecting her right eye where it meets the glass of the cop car.

The eyes of Paris Hilton. I read a gossip blog that ridicules one of her eyes for being "wonky." The blogger calls her "Wonky McValtrex." As a talisman I adore it. I adore saying the syllables: *Wonk-y Mc-Val-trex*. Looking at Ut's photo, though, I experience such radiant pathos for Paris that his tag for her sounds excessively mean. Wonky eyes crammed tight and sieving tears.

Where the line crops her eye and meets the glass of the cop car, a gleam of red—the flushed cheeks of Paris meet the red, swirling light of the juridical. The rouge, howling light of the police. When Alli and I lived on Shotwell Street, the guys on the street would always indicate the approach of a squad car by a shrill whine. Onomatopoetic neighborhood solidarity. "Mrs. Officer." But in the picture, what *is* the source of that light? The police? The paparazzi? The picture feels like it's being taken *in* the car, it's so close, highlighting the impossibility of proximity. The rest of the car is a kind of dull metallic gray, in slight contrast to Paris's cute jacket and total contrast to the thrumming reds and that bright light of warning.

The space between the back of Paris's head and the boy's jacket is in the exact shape of a black tornado. The gloomy tornado of squad car interior. Exactly bisecting the photo vertically, it makes the distance between her and the boys allegorical. *I fought the law and the law*....Well...The cop car itself is a metonymy for a world into which Paris is not prepared. I've relived her walk from the mansion to the car over and over, the whole walk made infinitely more uncomfortable by the din of photographers and reporters. Far from the mere translation of her body from the comfortable psychoarchitecture of the manor to the pre-prison confinement of the squad car's backseat, the walk in my mind represents the initial experience of the juridical in the life of Paris.

Obviously, on second thought, her whole life had been an experience of the juridical: as a very rich person whose money derives from the subjugation of slave labor around the world, she had of course experienced the juridical as it strove ceaselessly to protect and maintain her wealth and power. So this walk from the house to the car is actually a walk to the other side of the law. An intense translation, no doubt. And Paris Hilton is hardly the only person to burst into tears in a similar situation. I mean, *arrested*.

On Saturday I stood in front of *Paris Hilton* for twenty minutes or so. It felt like a long time, and soon I was looking just as much at the faces of people encountering the image. Nobody lingered for very long that I saw, but if there was any response it was generally a smile. An affirmation or memory perhaps of the spectacular event of Paris Hilton going to jail. But nothing extreme. No obvious displays of sympathy or pathos, no acknowledgement of Paris' pain. The affective response to the photograph of Phuc couldn't be more different. That photograph provokes an historical or imaginary recognition, a consensual feeling of horror. Together, the two feel like a catalogue of the abbreviated palette of contemporary expression: attraction, repulsion, steadfast ambivalence. Thumbs up, thumbs down, no comment.

On the night in 2001 that I decided to die, I walked around the city all night. First to the Golden Gate Bridge, which was to be the *mise en scene* for my departure from the living. I was picked up in the Tenderloin by a hooker who said she was looking for stray fish and was I stray fish. I said, I don't know. I didn't know. I walked in long orbits, like a hysterical planet staggering around the gravity of its star. I mean around the *bar* which I knew would open at 6 a.m.

The bar opened. It was Pearl Harbor Day, and the TV showed alternating images of George W. Bush commemorating the attacks (the first Pearl Harbor day after 9/11) with sequences from *Pearl Harbor* (2001, dir. Michael Bay.). I don't remember how I made it back to Jennifer's house. It was still "early." She buzzed me in and I walked up three flights of stairs to the apartment. I slumped down in the hallway and started crashing my head into the wall. Steve got up. Jennifer was crying and asked me what I wanted her to do. I told her call the hospital. Call and have them take me to the hospital.

Then two cops came and lay down on my back, cuffing me with the iconic plastic strap of protests and mass arrests. They took me back down the three flights of stairs and into the cop car. I was only barely aware that people were standing at their windows, tactfully or blatantly staring out of their windows. I had lived there for years, and they must have seen me dozens of times, some of them; maybe wondered what I did or how I lived; maybe some of them even saw Jennifer and I fucking in our bed, forgetting to draw the curtains closed. I wonder what painter's work our fucking resembled. Brueghel the Younger?

Steve got in the car and we went to the hospital. On the way there I begged the cops to shoot me with their guns. They told me to wait just a minute and things would be all right.

Baudelaire wrote a suicide note to his mother. His detractors would later call it an episodic melodrama typical of him. He would make fun of it himself later in life. In the note, he told his mom to give Jeanne a bunch of money. He said he was dying in great anxiety. He went to a café and ran a knife through his ribs and remembered nothing else until waking up in a police station. Was it all a dream? Then he went to live with his mom for a while and made her copy out his poems. When the inevitable falling out fell he told his friends he left because she served claret and he only drank Burgundy.

I'm *so* not trying to identify myself with Baudelaire in this translation. But the other morning when I was at the haute coffee shop I read this line of Baudelaire's: "I have cultivated my hysteria with delight and terror," and I thought, fuck, *that's sooooo me.* I guess I should just get it all out now? Okay. Like Baudelaire, I'm intensely chaste, waking up in the morning well before dawn to yell out my prayers into the night which is by gradations masking the twinklings of the stars. I speak perfect, jaded French. I'm "in love" with opiates. I occasionally entertain the fantasy of a dependentless and brief life. And I used to wear all black.

At least I don't *hate the stars.* Baudelaire may have hated them. Or, you know, he may have hated them sometimes. The character of Baudelaire's prose is that it contradicts itself all the time, collated as an *oeuvre,* sometimes within the same piece. In a comedic move, the oppositional instances of his thought are generally presented as polemical truths endlessly rooted in the canon of truth. A stellar pronouncement allergic to disaster. I wanted to brood on the stars in Baudelaire but the wires woven into my pores kept trembling with those sublime vibrations, someone reaching out.

Have you heard Paris Hilton's pop songs? There's recent-ish work, like "My BFF" and 2008's "Paris for President," but the real glittering diamond in her *oeuvre* is "The Stars are Blind." The central conceit of "Stars" is that *although* the stars are blind, there is still a potentiality for human intimacy and love, the condensation of agents into a totally innovative economy based on the reciprocity of generous feelings and attentive caresses. It reminds me of the post-script to Rob Halpern's *Disaster Suites,* in which Rob references Baudelaire and the idea that *Les Fleurs du Mal* is the first book of poems not "illuminated in starlight," i.e. the first book to have no destiny. Rob suggests that despite this lack of stellar or divine guidance, Baudelaire's poetry constitutes a promise, a resistance to the "death-in-life prescribed by a new world of commodities." *Even though the gods are crazy / Even though the stars are blind / If you show me real love baby / I'll show you mine.*

I can make it nice or naughty / be the devil or angel too. Baudelaire infamously wrote poems in praise of Satan. But Satan, just like the other stars, finds vacillating and provisional libidinal caricature in his work. The satanic is on one hand an allegory for radical nonconformity, including Baudelaire's unwillingness to "conform" to the emerging contours of contemporary French socialism. On the other hand, the satanic is associated with commerce, modes Baudelaire's poetry typically represents as an adverse aspiration. *Ad astra per aspera.*

It's not quite right to say that Satan is a star. Lucifer is a star, the star of morning. But even that tradition emerges out of total confusion. Some early Christian hymns describe Christ, not Satan, as the Morning Star. *Lucifer* just means whatever brings light. Baudelaire returns to the idea that humanity is living in a state of perpetual falling. Angels writhing around in excrement and cock rings...

In *Metamorphoses* by Ovid he describes Prometheus ordering the humans to look up to the stars, to reflect what they found there. Baudelaire, already compromised in his feelings about the sidereal, scoffs at the notion that the human face reflects the divine. Even, or especially, while undertaking the most sublime human experience (sex), the human face looks tortured, wrenched in many directions by shock and stress. My neighbors' faces half sobs and half shrieks, still as if stuck behind non-reflective glass or in the luminescent economy of photography. My face says what my hippocampus thinks. I talk with my mouth. Angelic clauses you could break out on Xmas they're so chaste.

I want to look out and see the stars and think they're a bulwark against the ambivalent feelings accompanying every spelunk into shopping. The rioters tap on the glass for instance. I see their rings shine, but do I love their destinies? I am their destiny, their critical stellar visage. But I'm stooped down, smelling gossip and trying to distill that into honeyed liquor.

Do you know that you can buy stars? Day or night they're for sale. For $50 or so you can name a star. You also get a beautiful 12" X 16" full color parchment certificate personalized with the star name, date and coordinates, a personalized 12" X 16" sky chart containing the star name, star date, the constellation and the location circled in red where the star is in the sky, a booklet on astronomy written by a professional astronomer with additional sky charts, and a letter of congratulations/memorial.

In *Paris Dream*, Baudelaire describes the experience of being ravished by an image that one cannot touch. It's too obscure, too hot, too distant. The auratic breathing flesh of Paris Hilton, the Latin Quarter saturated with dandies, bestbuy.com. It dreams a world vanquished of the vegetal irregular.

No trees, but endless stairs and escalators. Not the Ganges, but gift-wrapped trinkets made by slaves, gift-wrapped by slaves and circulated by slightly more privileged slaves. This is a holidays poem obviously.

Once, I dumped the ocean, but then I needed it. No star from anywhere, no vestige of the sun or the moon. The scene itself glows with its own fire. Night is the kairos for the plenitude of miracles the poem dreams. The fact that these spectacles are only for the eye, only in retrospect does it seem horrible. In "Dusk," night is the time for the worker to recollect on her daily work, i.e. even if the meaning vanishes, the working day obtains as work-without-work. Does this mean the end of night, if the universe is determined by the inversion of time? The intrusion of time into the dream. That is, the poem predicts the future abdication of the commodity even as it functions as a paean to production and commodities. Instant nostalgia.

Translation begins with stargazing. Looking at shapes, thinking about what to call everything that radiates out of objects at a great distance and of great enigma. Those stars with hair, interrupting the status quo catastrophe when their orbit permits, drawing up the eyes of the people whipping other people in the fields. The people being whipped by the other people in their fields. Their hairs whipped, trapped between the whip and the soft, smooth, angelic flesh of the back.

Places that exist without existing. Places like stars—you can't see them up close, they'd burn you so bad. The places that live like a language that died without dying. Still, it's like looking at a star. You know when you see a star you're looking at light that's like a million years old. The Paris I go to in 2010 is not Baudelaire's Paris, or Louise Michel's or Norma's—yet it is, in translation.

The mall far from flowering now appears to have aspired to appear as pure spirit. The tanks inside which slaves stitch "Hanes" on your Hanes persist in reality however, engulfing the flora and fauna which once crept over even the *rue Rivoli*.

For this translation, I've decided that I know French. I don't "know French," i.e. I've never studied French. And I don't know the grammatical rules of sentence structure and my vocabulary is critically impoverished. And if you handed me a page with French words on it, like a poem by Charles

Baudelaire, and asked me to tell you what it "means" I won't be able to really tell you. And yet I will be able to read it, and I will be able to tell you what it's like, and what it's saying. This is a paradox that the poem is *totally in love with,* but not so much the cheese monger when I'm saying, "half of it s'il vous plait" or when I'm telling a waitress that I'll have "maybe *fromage."* In fact nothing is more annoying, and they say undecipherable things in response that make my chaste cheeks burnish.

On our first day in Paris, Alli and I went to go see Charles Baudelaire's grave in the Cemetiere Montparnasse. They buried Baudelaire with his stepfather, who he "esteemed," i.e. hated guts. Baudelaire's casket is on top of Aupick's and Baudelaire's mom's is on top of his. The chastest possible accumulation of bodies in cramped space. It's so fucked up it's inspiring.

Walking out of the cemetery in daylight bright and crisp as a drying photo of, oh…Khloe Kardashian, we headed for the exit. I heard a noise behind us, and we turned around and saw a pigeon drop out of a tree, rocklike in its gravitas. You don't look in the sky and expect a star to disembed from its niche in the blackness and streak across your field of vision, and likewise you don't expect a bird to fall instead of fly out of a tree. I thought that bird just fucking died and dropped out of a tree in the Cemetiere Montparnasse. I went over to check it out, and it wasn't dead, but obviously dying. The throes marked by the inability to be what you are, i.e., what makes a bird a bird is its never having to *fall.*

It seemed pretty bad to see such a thing in a cemetery of all places. But I didn't really think about it much until our last day when we went to Pere Lachaise. It was drizzling as we approached but the drops stopped. The stones were slick though and we walked slowly through them. Striding by Gertrude Stein and Alice B., Wilde's germy rock, treading closely to the map to avoid the hordes groping towards Morrison. We decided to leave and as we turned a corner we found ourselves alone, not surrounded by any other cemetery tourists.

We had been making these jokes, whenever we walked by a grave whose façade was chipped to permit a peek into the darkness they enclosed, that the dead were waking and stirring to pursue us. But we weren't *really* scared until we turned this corner and found ourselves alone on the wet stones and saw a dry cat standing on top of one of the graves. The cat stared at us and its lashes hissed. As we walked by, both of us shut up and stared intently at the cat. It followed us with its eyes. Even as we inched away from the convolute of graves we felt it looking at us.

Now the paranoia went into overdrive. Two instances of bizarre animal behavior attendant upon leaving two cemeteries. The bird debirded, plunked out of the nest and onto the sidewalk. The fierce, old cat appearing from below, menacing our attempt to escape the land of the dead. Before I left, Bruce told me to be on the lookout for omens, and now his words resounded in my mind. That night, in between consciousness and dreams, I kept imagining myself inside that bird, now a metonymy for the three airplanes we'd soon be boarding, dropping out of the sky. So unnatural. If God had wanted airplanes to fall out of the sky he wouldn't have inspired human geniuses to fabricate wings.

But if it had to be my last day on Earth, I would go screaming into star-hot contact with the earth satiate of fattened duck livers, *gamay nouveau,* and poetry, the flutter-inducing auratic residue of *living translation.* Anyway the planes didn't crash. We drank caraway seed schnapps and ate lamb sandwiches and watched *My Cousin Vinny* (1992, dir. Jonathan Lynn)and 20 hours or so later landed in Oakland. Two days later I went back to work and it felt as if the trip to Paris had barely happened. A tiny interruption in a conditional life slowly cognizant of its own imprisonment. A weekend, only far more resplendent of fattened duck livers, *gamay nouveau,* and poetry. It felt like a dream. Was it all a dream?

FUTURE PERFECT

A cyberpunk memoir for David and Sara

Every epoch sings its future one. —Michelet

I'm working for the future, cause I live in a computer. —Lil B

CHAPTER ONE *ANARCHIST LUNCH*

When I told Chris that I was cooking a goat heart he said *that's
so Satanic.*

The conventional story of translation is one of maligned agency. Somebody
purports to control a kind of knowledge which permits access to
incomprehensible phrases. Knowledge, always of *something rather evil.*
Tempting forms of life into glossolalic revolution. But just as much as a
translator defaults on her statist duty by this wicked praxis, a vulnerable
patiency makes her form of life permeable.
Liable to feedback. So no wonder while translating the poems in
Les Fleurs du Mal even my *hors d'oeuvres* litanized Lucifer.

I took the train down the Ferry Building farmer's market. Jackqueline
shucked oysters from afar but I didn't go say hi. When I go to the market I
am transformed into an effluvial impatience machine, radiating disdain for
my colleagues in consumption, instantly irritated by their slightest
retardations or aggravating hesitations in which variety of wild mushroom
spore they'd like to buy. I didn't want to out myself as such a dick to Jack. I
imagined myself wafting from stall to stall with the grace of Mila Kunis in
Black Swan (2010, dir. Darren Aronofsky.)

But even with such delusional ease, I hesitated in front of the goat heart. I
wanted to cook it for my banquet, but could I cook it? Would my guests
barf? I know that my rural, white, petit bourgeois parents would utterly
barf. I bought the heart.

You know how deToqueville wasn't able to even *see* working-class French
people until 1848? What do you think he thought about
lobsters? Those vermillion, crap-eating, delicious bugs. In San
Francisco, parts of animals like goat heart have become the choice kinds of
things to eat for bourgeois foodies. The gentrification of offal eating evokes
their desperate attempt to embody something freaky in their lives. As if
eating lamb kidneys offset the banality of the cognitariat tech job and the
Montessori splurge. It's reductive to mock the bourgeois like this, I know.
Immature, useless, finally hypocritical. Welcome to the world of Charles
Baudelaire.

Tony came over, then Cynthia, and then Lauren and Stephanie, from the radical ladies clothing swap at Sara's. I melted butter over medium-high heat until the bubbles subsided. I set the goat heart in the pan, gave it one shake so nothing would stick and let the butter brown the purple surface of each piece. I waited a minute or two, smelling the butter and the slightly sweet aroma of roasting heart.

I was nervous. Was it going to make everybody barf? Was I going to barf?

I made a tiny bed of puntarella in the middle of each plate, flanked by small pieces of goat, triangulated by a wedge of lemon. We all filled our glasses with rosé made the edges sing. Whenever I cook something I've never made before, especially something I'm unsure about, I always wait until somebody else tastes it before trying it. It's the closest my paranoia comes to Napoleon's, although like him I'm also white and wealthy. The consensus was that the goat heart was okay. I liked it too.

The luncheon was decadent and pleasant. Everybody was in a really good mood and seemed to like the courses as they came. We had a salad with purple asparagus, frisee, wild boar lardons, and parmesan. And I made a pan-seared sea bass with an endive, tarragon, and grape marmalata. And a roast loin of pork with fennel, and orzo with asparagus and lots of parmesan. And delicious lemon thyme shortbreads and blueberries and mango with orange juice for dessert. And we drank the rosé, and two bottles of white wine, and a bottle of red wine, and then we went to see the Invisible Committee at the anarchist space on 16th and Mission.

CHAPTER TWO *AT THE ANARCHIST SPACE*

I had worried for a week about what to wear to see the Invisible Committee, but the pork took a little longer than I thought and I had to wear my banquet swag. Brown boots, black jeans, Vivian Girls
t-shirt, big blue glasses. I put on a light blue summer blazer and we all walked over to the space.

None of us had been to the anarchist space before, so we wandered a little bit around the BART station, by the black plantains in the market stall, in the crosswalk, in the warm and druggie ambience of the plaza. It had been conceptually challenging to imagine our destination being in the Mission at all. My neighborhood had been strollerized long enough to make the existence of an anarchist space improbable. On the other hand, if it was going to be anywhere in the Mission, this intersection was appropriate. Junkies and rascals teemed by the escalators. The very junkies and rascals which had made the neighborhood cheap in the 1990s and who had been systematically evacuated since the .com boom. Which all feels like it happened "a hundred years ago," so the present day BART plaza provokes nostalgia, with all the sorrow that that word contains.

The room was packed. It felt like a punk show, that glamorous anticipation of imminent negative glee. The three young members of the Invisible Committee sat in a row of chairs in front, next to the two moderators and two unidentified men in their 50s. Somebody played music on an I-Pod while everybody up front sat in silence. People chattered and their chatter was gleeful and negative, their skin was almost always white and under 30. I was the only one wearing a light blue summer blazer and I was glad I didn't really wear the seersucker shorts and boat shoes as I had threatened.

The music stopped and a surly young man came and addressed the crowd. He explained that the space was private and promised to kick anybody out at any time for any reason. He also said that the space was a
law-enforcement-free zone and anybody who was law enforcement had to leave. Then he said they had a blog and a Facebook, which seemed kind of funny following the boast to privacy and withering proscription of law enforcement.

Only one of the three young French people spoke. He never used the pronoun "I," but always "we." The talk was good, reiterating many of the themes in *The Coming Insurrection,* the call to arms that so many of us have been reading over the last year or so. But it got more complicated when questions were opened up to the audience. The spokesperson seemed to misunderstand or resent every question, although his charisma was such that this felt more charming than bratty. People wanted to know did they really advocate bringing down the state. They said yes. People wanted to know why they disdained the Marxist critique of political economy. They seemed frustrated and they said we came here to talk about civil war, not about Marxism.

Finally, someone remarked about their insistence on not using the singular personal pronoun. The person said that here in America we think about resistance to oppression often in terms of identity, in terms of racial identity, or gender, or queerness. The spokesperson paused and the whole room casually and glamorously shuddered. He said "I really have to pee."

CHAPTER THREE *TO THE BOURGEOIS*

Walking around Paris we saw the posters on the subway, at the bus stops, on telephone poles, on the sides of walls. The famous photograph by Lizzie Himmel from 1985, *Basquiat In His Studio,* plastered the city. We saw the posters several times before we figured out that there was a huge Basquiat show at the Musee d'Art Moderne.

In the photo, taken when Basquiat was 24, the painter sits in a red chair with metal arm rests. The red of the back is split by a yellow rectangle, and the chair's identical twin lies on the ground horizontally, used as a footrest. The beauty of his suit is offset by the chalky dust of the hems and the shock of his bare feet. He's holding a paint brush in his right hand like a lawn dart. He looks utterly intense and absolutely chill.

One thing you can never tell about Basquiat is the money thing. There's a real ambiguity to the narrative, so that at times he's firmly established as a bourgeois artist, and at other times, conversely, his poverty is privileged. All accounts agree that when he did start making enormous sums of money from selling his paintings he was very liberal, spending it all on very fine suits and heroin for him and all his comrades.

Baudelaire wrote the *Salon of 1846* when *he* was 24. "To The Bourgeois" is a kind of preface to the *Salon,* a long review of contemporary painting full of praise (Delacroix), blame (Vernet), threats and warnings to the state and their battalions; praises and paeans to the state and their battalions; love for the bourgeois, scorn for the bourgeois, etc. Which makes understanding the meaning of the few paragraphs that open his book difficult to pin down. You know the bliss of hearing dance music on cocaine, and the hell of 12 hours later? That kind of somatic range, sublated into five paragraphs of prose, ruthlessly ironic, dazzlingly laudatory.

The week before we went to Paris there had been massive protests all over France. Rail had been shut down, freeways had been closed down, service connecting the city to the airport stopped. Alli and I worried as these protests continued in intensity up to the day of our flight from Reykjavik to Paris. We were inside a crisis of solidarity. We were in *luv* with the protests, no question. We wanted the fascist Sarkozy government eradicated. We wanted the students of Paris, hand in hand with the working class, to organize, and establish a confederation based on consensus and *egalite*. We also wanted to check in our hotel and eat fresh baked croissants and wash down *epoisses* with red wine from Bourgogne. You know how in *Confessions* St. Augustine says like *Lord give me chastity...but not yet!?*

By the time we got to Paris, the activity had mostly died down. We were able to get on the RAF train from CDG and take it to our cheap hotel room near the Louvre. We sat by the Seine for a picnic, *so* like the bourgeois of late 19th century painting. We bought a piece of Alsatian Muenster, a baguette, country pate, an éclair, and a bottle of Gamay Nouveau. I scraped away crumbs off of my pants and found the museum on the map.

We stopped for a coffee and a Gauloises. Above us, a massive memorial artwork to Michael Jackson was installed on the wall of the Palais d'Tokyo. The image was Jackson's face behind big dark sunglasses and black leather jacket with upturned collar. The Jackson of *Bad*, although he had a big smile on his face, not the menacing glare of the album cover. The piece was made out of segments of masking tape, black and white, running vertical and horizontal. Below the image of the face, also with tape, his dates: 1958-2009. Basquiat was born in 1960.

After coffee we looked around for the entrance, but then we saw the queue. The line snaked out of the entrance to the museum, down the stairs, and along a cast-iron gate that stretched as far as we could see. How long did it go? We started walking parallel to the line. After a block we began negotiations concerning were we going to wait in this line. When we got two blocks deep we turned around and started walking back to the Metro and decided to come back the next morning when the museum opened at 10:00.

I made Alli get up at 8:00 the next morning so we could shower, drink coffee, have a croissant, and make it to the museum to be early in the line. We couldn't find anything excellent in the way of patisseries by the Museum so ended up at a kind of Parisian Starbucks where we had pain au chocolat and espresso that came out of a pushbutton machine. We got to the museum and the already-lengthening line by 9:30. There weren't that many tourists. There were old couples, packs of feral teens, lovers in their 20s and 30s. Everybody seemed to smoke. We waited, not-quite caffeinated enough and semi-squabbling from having to rush out of the hotel that morning.

At 5 minutes til 10 a flatbed truck rolled up and about a dozen people jumped out of the back. They were carrying huge banners that stretched across the shoulders of two or three of them at a time. They charged up the round stairs of the museum and blocked the entrance. The one who appeared to be their leader had a megaphone and started chanting. The rest followed along. He looked like one of the drunken beadles in Courbet's *Burial at Ornans*, which might have endeared me more to him at the time had I been better slept.

I watched with a little bit of fascinated curiosity, since I'm a wealthy white American, and in America, before Occupy, we didn't protest austerity measures and unemployment *we exported them*. As the people in front of us in line scattered in unison, we stood, confused. Surely, having caused a bit of a row at the art museum, these protestors would now move on to some more critically strategic location and permit us to be admitted into the museum to view the Basquiat paintings on exhibit. *Mais non.*

When we finally gave up and sulked back to the Metro for the second time in two days, I said some of the stupidest things imaginable to Alli. I said fuck those protestors, let the capitalists win, just let us go in and see those Basquiats. It was funny, but was it funny ha ha? I really did want a suspension of insurrectionary activity—even for two hours— so that my vacation could rule this much harder: a shameful longing for picnolepsis inside the frenzy of a kairos. Oinking pig in me. It's been like this my whole life.

CHAPTER FOUR *1977*

The first cells of my honky brain organized into lumps in 1977, the year of premonitions that Franco "Bifo" Berardi describes as paradoxically the end of all 20ᵗʰ century utopias and a year which somehow persists as the year that "will always be around the corner," the coming revolution. It was a year whose double numbers were read widely as a sign of the imminent apocalypse. That anticipation infected pop music, from Bowie's "Five Years" to Culture's "Two Sevens Clash." It was the year Marcus Garvey forecast the end of white domination.

The mantra of that time was that in order to have fun you have to have no fun, to have feelings you have to have no feelings. To have a future you have to have no future. Bifo on 1977: "The memory of that year has not been cancelled, because hope in a world where friendship prevails over competition and joy prevails over oppression cannot be cancelled."

Punk temporality is precisely that of the prolonged moment of negative immediacy, which makes its suggestions of progressive political activism, saturated with utopian imagination, appear as stasis and abjection. Sex Pistols is a band, but also a furious contradiction inside fashion, itself simultaneously politics, discontent to be thought solely in either term as such.

So Sex Pistols epitomizes the paradoxical erotic optics of pop spectacle in all forms that appear after 1977: simultaneous loathing and sublimation. Simultaneously directed at ecstasy and masochistic. Four infantile dandies, hybrid James Dean and Ulrike Meinhoff. They embody a two-fingered rejection of iconic control, yet they themselves are unable to usurp their own evil genius puppetmaster except by dissolution and untimely death. They don't play their instruments, and they don't play concerts or write songs, and yet their name emblazons one of the truly perfect pop albums ever made.

CHAPTER FIVE *PUNK ROCK*

I'm hardly able to embrace an invasive self-identification with the "poet" but ironically in my first incarnation as a baby dandy, I had no trouble subscribing to an unquestioned social hierarchy. So quantifiable that we had a system which calculated "punk points." Staying up all night playing Risk and drinking coffee contributed to one's cache of punk points, going to class or work brought about a loss. I've depleted my hoard. But because I *had* been punk, when Ted asked everybody in the room at Small Press Traffic to raise their middle fingers and yell *Fuck capitalist hegemony!* extending the finger felt like returning to some long-inhabited experience of digital lengthening.

The "punk scene" and the "poetry community," dwell in very different sets of temporal epistemology. Great works of punk art tend to absorb into the "eternal present" of pop music. Complicated of course by punk's own rich historicity, emerging as a mature art form in 1977, the inception of an already-finished moment we hope hasn't ended yet. This may help explain the indestructibility of punk fashion, which otherwise has to be read as a nostalgia only peculiar in its persistence and homogeneity.

Poetry communities are mostly made up of poets who like to think of "poetry" as a historical form of art, made of writing, that goes back many thousands of years. So the metrical narrative epics that ancient Greek society used as a tribal encyclopedia are subsumed into an expanding historical continuum that includes the very text you are reading right now. Funny, right?

In punk scenes, the institutional memory, especially given its members are 13-24, is abbreviated and thus every entrance or departure from a lived place is greeted with greater hysteria or more perfectly affected ambivalence. The betrayals, rifts, toxic people and toxic behaviors, incessant worrying over the scene itself—all this happens because it's finally just people who make these communities—people living in a rotting and degraded socius inflected by a madness for competition.

When you're in a punk scene you contend too with the inherent paradox of negativity of its art. Canonical punk works formally embrace negativity for this expenditure of a surfeit of glee. The Sex Pistols proposed no fun, no feelings and no future. And yet their artwork was precisely fun, full of the most potent and shallow/deep feelings. And most curious of all is the choral finale of "God Save The Queen." That repetition of "Noooooooooo Fuuuuuuuuuture" proves to be a robust declaration allergic to dissolution by futurity. Because I was punk, I found myself repeatedly embedded in these conundrums. We would engage in collective activity and non-cash-based transactional hand-over economies all the time and then we would say fuck hippies.

We worried about the scene incessantly. We worried about questions of collective action against the hegemonic structures we knew most perverted our world. We hadn't read *Kapital* by Karl Marx but we did have the intuition that "growing up," i.e. practicing wage labor for survival, was what compelled one's transition from being in the punk scene to not being in it. So when Ted asked everyone to extend their middle fingers and yell *Fuck Capitalist Hegemony!* I said a form of something I had been saying since I was a child. I wanted to say it felt the same. And yet…

CHAPTER SIX *POST PUNK*

Frederic Jameson describes the "ambivalences" of the Utopian text.
Essentially, under capitalism, our "imaginations are hostages to our own
mode of production." So a Utopian project which asserts a radical difference
from current conditions is realized in proportion to its being imaginable.

But he also considers this ambivalence ontologically. Using the episteme of
"the trace," which expresses a dialectical presence from the past in the
present, just over the crest of legibility, Jameson exposes the
uni-directionality of this frame. The "trace," if it can be thought, could be
thought in relation to the other end of time, that is, the future. He writes,
"Utopia, which combines the not-yet being of the future with a textual
existence in the present is no less worthy of the archaeologies we are willing
to grant to the trace."

When I stopped being punk I quickly gathered to my bosom a vast amount
of debt. I started working a job that conformed to the normative temporal
arrangement of capitalist cognitariat life, the *working life* which could be
parceled into the working month, the working week made up of working
days, themselves arranged like *bricolage,* wink and you'll miss…*ichor welling
up* so much like the pus in a wound, that mushy uggy goody stuff. One
thing that happened right away is Sunday became really depressing.

CHAPTER SEVEN *SUNDAY DUSK*

It's true that my culture was trying to tell me my whole life that Sunday, and especially Sunday at dusk, was a gloomy time haunted by a ghost from its own future. Evan turned me on to Billie Holiday's "Gloomy Sunday," in which Sunday is the occasion for the mind to turn to contemplating suicide in order to reunite with a dead lover. David told me about Morrissey's "Every Day Is Like Sunday," which in typical Morrissean terms considers the quotidian "silent and grey," and Sunday the epitome of grisly quietude. The general despair of Sunday dusk is hyperbolized in Morrissey's melodramatic call for Armageddon, his pained plea for the eschatological event.

But beyond the regime of pop prophecies, consider that Sunday night convenes the blues typical of any period following intense communal ecstasy. I'm talking about church and, for several months out of the year in America, football. I had missed a lot of these cues, always having found church to be a brutal course in concentrated ennui and football the background noise for the naps the men in my family took on countless Sunday while the women in my family washed their spit off of plates.

In 2002, though, I watched football every Sunday. I would wake up and walk over to Clayton Street where John and I would start watching football at 10 in the morning. Sometimes Steve or Matthew watched with us. We were poor so we'd walk to the liquor store and buy 40 oz. beers for $2 and drink them on the couch and chainsmoke.

We were faithful to the Raiders that season. It wasn't just fealty to the semi-local; they were good that year. Every time the Raiders scored points we'd put on Ice Cube's "Wrong Nigga To Fuck Wit." *Goddamn it's a brand new payback / from the straight gangsta mack in straight gangsta black.* And we'd dance with delight at the prowess of the Raiders, the sublime fury of Cube, our youthful *j'ne sais quoi*. But eventually the football games would end and on the West Coast it would still be sort of early. We'd all be deranged with booze and really ought to have all passed out but it felt too early. So we'd cohabitate in a haze of almost entirely liquidated excitation, settling into a soft melancholy.

Is it a coincidence that the day of the week specifically given over to Christian worship was also the chosen day for terrifying nationalist spectacular aggression in game form? In the beginning of Christianity, there must have been some fierce debate about whether or not it was okay to go watch the gladiators fight wild animals in the arenas in Rome. Tertullian wrote a whole book, *De Spectaculis,* considering the question. For Tertullian, it was not okay for Christians to watch the games and contests; they were for heathens by heathens, and to put your body in the company of heathens watching heathens in competition, stirring all that bile and mushy ichor, even a true Christian would slump away a little heatheny when the whistle blew. Since the association of the day Sunday with the worship of Jesus, it's been a fraught and overdetermined temporal zone for everyone in the West who affirms the working week and whose practices thus take shape in deference to Sunday.

It's this ideological force of Sunday as an overdetermined time that keeps Sunday counterrevolutionary. In a critique of Marx's limited exposition of time, Giorgio Agamben writes, "Every conception of history is invariably accompanied by a certain experience of time which is implicit in it, conditions it, and thereby has to be elucidated…the original task of a genuine revolution, therefore, is never mere to 'change the world' but also—and above all—to change time." As is well known, one of the first things republicans did in the French revolution was change the calendar.

So as for the weekend, everybody's working for it. But if we like the weekend so much, and I am led to believe that "we" do like it very much, why don't we refuse en masse to accept its termination? What if we collectively demand that the "weekend," the afterlife of that temporal category of production, the "week," be extended in its relation to that time of production?

The anticipation for the weekend extends as a series of anticipatory decisions and premonitions, but the weekend doesn't start before a clear peal, the bell sounding the factory closed. In contrast, the gloom of Sunday can emerge at any moment, without any obvious cause.

Sunday contains its own homuncular Sunday, establishing a threshold which marks the end of that long-hoped-for weekend and the initiation of something different, something sinister, something dreadful. Which is to say that by the almost imperceptible crossing of some temporal boundary, Sunday dusk becomes Monday morning.

How Robert Duncan would it be to say that this gloom is a psychic form of time travel. That the discomfort, the resentment, the longing wrapped inside gauze, all of the expended energy and woe results in a holler back from future time, administrating the disappearing present, checking the relish of the crepuscular waning of the sometimes long and sometimes short second day of the weekend.

CHAPTER EIGHT *FRIDAY*

As things stand, the weekend obtains as an allegorical miniature of all time free from the site of one's labor. And if Sunday is the compromised space marking the decline and fall of this life-saving temporality, then its ascending counterpart on the other end of time is obviously Friday. The death of the weekend is the moment at which one can no longer feel as if it were Friday. The bodies piling up in the afterlife of history. The "Friday" of a sane modernism seems irrecuperable, and that loss is mourned by critical piece of cultural art this year in America, Rebecca Black's "Friday."

The central assertion of "Friday" is a) that it's Friday and b) that one has a responsibility to certain kinds of praxis given that fact.

The uncanny thing about the first assertion of "Friday" is that, far from being inane or obvious, to call a time Friday is essentially to prophesize. The revelation of Friday also implies the instantiation of Sunday, however far in the distance, a chronological and ideological inevitability that Black affirms with her often-mocked bridge, *the next day is Saturday / after that is Sunday.*

In the same way that there are miniature Sundays that tend to strike with all their dolor and wrath on Sunday (but can happen any time,) there are also simulacral Fridays that crack through the waning work day. But after the inception of the consensual moment known as Friday, everyone has a little bit of a stretched smile on their face and sometimes they say Happy Friday. When I got the job that conformed to the normative temporal arrangement of capitalist cognitariat life, I would always grimace when people would say Happy Friday. A kind of quiver in anticipation of that short and fucked leash. The antithesis of the gloom that awaits anybody on Sunday dusk. The inception of an *afterward.*

But the ethical responsibility, articulated by Black as "got to get down on Friday," is comprised of a call to recognize the kairotic depth of the temporal moment which the annunciation of Friday initiates, a depth to some extent fraught in advance by the imminence of Sunday. *Tomorrow is Saturday / and Sunday comes afterward.*

I read the song as a tale of labor under contemporary conditions of production, and the fact that Black describes this in terms of the "learning day" makes little difference. The "learning day" is a kind of true preparatory experience for hegemonic, chronocentric servitude. *Then they put you on the day shift.*

CHAPTER NINE *THE RAPTURE*

Rapture mania didn't reach its full pitch until the week just before it was supposed to occur. There were occasional jokes about the billboards, semi- to total incredulity upon hearing the news for the first time. Is this what it was like to encounter a gossip from Jerusalem after they killed Jesus? Someone telling you, with the straightest of faces, *so...you know that freak folk dude from Nazareth that they crucified last week? Well I heard...* In San Francisco the people's response to the rapture's declaration was predictable: the exhortation of "Friday" found riotous expression in the primordial reception of the rapture: *partying partying yeah! Fun fun fun fun.*

The rapture was supposed to happen at 6:00 p.m. on Saturday, May 21. But because the financiers who run capitalist commerce have determined that the time of life on earth has to be parceled into regular and recognizable time zones to help maintain the easy flow of commodities around the world, "Saturday at 6:00" began in the Bay Area on Friday night.

The rapture parties signified a massive reconsideration of desires founded upon the bracing imminence of the end of time. I wasn't able to go to any of them. I had to work the commencement ceremony at the college where I work. We had to arrive at 10:30 and none of us had to do anything until 1:00. None of us failed to feel the significance of this wasted weekend time. To distract ourselves from insurrectionary fantasies, we talked about the rapture. We all agreed that if the rapture was truly coming, the last place any of us would want to be was at work. We eyed the students nervously as they started storming the football field.

I remembered sitting in church Sunday after Sunday and experiencing the most charged imaginative flights. In one fantasy, I commandeered a tiny aircraft. The aircraft was so small as to be invisible to the naked eye. If I so chose, I could signify my presence by casting a half-dollar size black hole, the negative black light of which would show my coordinates to the concerned. With my eyes I traced all the crannies and nooks of the church through which I'd soar, choosing to listen or not listen to the sermon. The most special feature of my miniature was that the smallest pieces of food could be translated into their regular-world size. I could live off one Arbys for weeks.

These reveries were a response to a boredom that is perhaps disappearing from this world. A profound incarceration minus prostheses. At the commencement ceremony everybody was constantly plucking away at their phones. The speakers droned. I sat in the back and felt my neck burn and vaguely thought of checking my own machine to make absolutely sure there hadn't been any catastrophic earthquakes in New Zealand, in which case I'd immediately head off to a riotous debauch of sex, opiates, grilled chicken livers, epoisses, aged Riesling.

When it was over, Alli and I went out for dinner at a Thai restaurant we had always made fun of because it was called Thai Stick. Then we saw *Bridesmaids* (2011, dir. Paul Feig) and celebrated the failure of end time activity by laughing hysterically for two hours in a dark room with a hundred people.

Sunday comes afterward. I spent the next day at Sara and David's. We studied Sanskrit, and then we studied Greek, and then we studied Spanish. After Spanish, we went out for Korean food and then Chris Daniels gave a talk with Chris Chen at Brian's. Chris and Chris both detailed tactics aimed at derailing this machine of global death we're all helping drive. Afterwards we splayed across the stoop and drank beers. We talked and laughed. Sunday turned into Monday. For the most part friendship prevailed over competition and joy prevailed over oppression. I went to bed sort of tipsy but not very gloomy for once. I thought this will have been a happy occasion for the writing coming afterward.

FUSEES 22

Fireworks...that is what we're selling, Lemon. Spectacle. It's what people want. The Romans knew it, Louis Quattorze knew it, Wolfowitz knows it. —Jack Donaghy, *30 Rock*

If the apocalypse comes then beep me.
—Buffy Summers, *Buffy the Vampire Slayer*

The world is coming to an end
and all I hear are fireworks bursting
in air like what's that song? Fuck I hate
fireworks. The only thing worse than
fireworks are real bombs, which is aggravatingly Platonic I
know. Moreover, a terrible paradigm for translation. Like, the
only thing worse than my translation of "Fusees 22" is
Baudelaire's *poem* "Fusees 22." An awful and sort of true
paradigm. Sort of true like everything awful. My friend died and
then I watched
Brokeback Mountain and stared at a tuna slab.
Outside fireworks streaked the sky,
a violent display of celebration, excessive
antithesis to my stupefied, untranslatable grief.

It's like getting fucked on September 11th:
awesome, morose, unforgettable. The world
is coming to an end, but that's just grammatical certainty
coming again to bear on temporal contingency.
The world is closing. The sentence is closing. The poem
is closing. The mall, the video store, the bookstore
is closing. And yet everything seems open for business,
entrenched as stasis amidst collapse.
It's like Dirty Harry's finger on the trigger in the opening
sequence of *Magnum Force,* an ambient
stability, desperately prolonging the inevitable
thrust of explosive release. It's like looking at a ship,
moored in glimmering bywater. I stand on the pier
and throw pesos as far as I can towards its rotten
lee. That would have been me, skimming the moss. A few weeks after
September 11th, I went to defenestrate myself from the horror of
lumpenbourgeois romantic reversal. I was half rich and all miserable,
hysterical about my beautiful misery and how much I wanted it to die. Do
amoebas want to get tickled or stay napping? What do you think?
When I was ten I called the record store in the city
to ask if they had a copy of the first Guns N' Roses EP
Live Like A Suicide. I called with the inchoate fever
that follows the encounter with a life-changing piece
of art, by which I mean *Appetite for Destruction* had given

me an appetite for cultural mastery over the *oeuvre*
of GNR. A male voice answered. I squeaked,
do you have *Live* (rhymes with "shiv") *Like A Suicide*
by Guns N' Roses? He said, do you mean *Live* (rhymes with "jive")
Like A Suicide? We don't have that. I went intowhite mourning.
That sounds like a snobby move on his part, and it sort of was.
But also he was doing me a favor. It's like the first time I ordered a
café avec crème in Paris and I pronounced it "cream" to which the waiter
oozed back, *crhemh.* Anyway, both pronunciations
of *Live Like a Suicide* effect a melodramatic paradox, like a scalding
avalanche. A few days after I didn't jump my ribs into glass,
Steve Silberman saw me on Cole Street and told me I was too young to
commit suicide. I could do it when I was 40. I vaguely understood that
my amoebal psyche hadn't *earned* its death drive. And god, what if I
had done it!? I would have never met Alli, never met Dana,
never seen *Bridesmaids.*

Boom. Kaboom. Bombs of sheer report. Bombs that make
minimalist paintings.
We'd hear gunshots any season and Alli or I would say, *fireworks?*
A classic joke to distract us from the aural prompt to sensible
fear. Cottonmouth as long as life so the question comes, why live?
To go into business to humiliate your dad?
To revenge your abrasive and pathetic childhood by fucking
someone for a pendant? Anyway, I can't qualify
for a small business loan and I haven't seen a pendant
flash for weeks. It's like my wealth, broad
as it is, still knows pixel precarity.
The rulers are fashioning a rhetoric of hope
and my Marxist friends are doing the same. They're hoping
that the historically murderous firecracker known as
capitalism has an abbreviating fuse. Is about to burst
and sift into ash. I hope it bursts too. And yet
afterwards I want to meet you all for brunch
and watch you spray syrup over eggy wheat.
Which I know makes me quite simply a vestigial, conflicted,
complacent neoliberal pig. I'm working on it. My cracked oink
follows hot on your alarm clock, that murderer of dreams. But I
don't want *anyone* to eat trash. Sometimes on

the walk to work I eye those piles of food on the corner,
mysterious in their excess, ostensibly delicious
despite their dislocation. It's a struggle not to put my
snout inside the noodles and sniff it up. And then
say it's cause I hate litter. It's like as a kid on July 5th
I walked around picking up the paper casings from
so many firecrackers. Wretched, sweet gunpowder
residue. Then I'd go home and throw them in the
air like they were gold coins. It's like John Donne in
Lovers Infinitenesse where he invests in a stock
market of love with sighs, oaths, and letters
and finds his returns disappointing. But returns,
as the history of that very bloody capitalism shows us, over and
over, are never assured. I think of that trace from the other end of
time, hoping it's going to guide me like starlight guides some
hapless pilot. In *Fusees 22*, Baudelaire's sense of certainty about
the imminent end of the world determines the pace of his gait. So
he slouches on a café brick loading his pipe, judging
everybody's outfits. And, what is the
same thing, everybody's poetry. Poetry
so pretty it tells the future. I look at the stars, but they're just as
dumb as poetry. Pretty dumb. It's like holding onto a
firecracker in your hand, trying to be braver
than the flame sucking fuse. Pretty
dumb. Like writing a poem that wags
into prophecy. Sorry to make my poem
an *hors d'oeuvre*. One soggy with slimy dejecta.
Sorry to draw you all into my quasi-suicidal translation.
Too hard and too stupid all at once.
I'd love to feed you all *hors d'oeuvres*. To get that groan out of
you, to make it *so* unambiguous that the prosthetic hegemony of
feelinglessness gives up on us. Woods of perpetual orgasm in
which I age and rear. Woods in which we kiss each other's
tweets. Smile at the salt of them. I know this poem causes you
the most delicious, profound disappointment. But I'm going to
leave it just as it is. Like some long-abandoned mall on the peripheries of a
long-abandoned Midwestern city. A mall named after a long-murdered tribe
of aboriginal Americans. Or like that Olympic lacrosse stadium we saw
outside of Athens. Greeks don't play lacrosse, it turns out. But they do

gather in the streets. They wear gloves to protect their respiratory systems against tear gas. They throw glass. Glass breaking on a wall of gassy pork. It's like black cats spraying off inside a frog. It's like M80s bursting in the Missouri air, toad-like spraying ash over meth labs. A laundry ever after. A laundry list of things in this book that beg me to cross them out. With glitter lipstick on, bragging at a mirror. But I'm going to leave all this error in the book. Smeared all over its pages, wet with Satanic fizzy water. All the monsters and lies and horny swans with booger-capped talons. Because I want to set an exact date to my ~~sadness~~ anger.

Roof Books

the best in language since 1976

Selected & Recent Titles

- Craig Dworkin. **Motes**. 88 p. $14.95
- Nada Gordon. **Scented Rushes**. 104 p. $13.95
- Joel Kuszai. **Accidency**. 120 p. $14.95.
- Evelyn Reilly. **Apocalypso**. 112 p. $14.95
- Anne Tardos. **Both Poems**. 112 p. $14.95
- Edwin Torres. **Yes Thing No Thing**. 128 p. $14.95.
- César Vallejo. **Against Professional Secrets**.
Translated by Joseph Mulligan.
(complete Spanish/English) 104 p. $14.95.
- Wellmen, Mac. **Split the Stick: A Minimalist-Divan**. 96 p. $14.95

Roof Books are published by
Segue Foundation
300 Bowery • New York, NY 10012
Visit our website at seguefoundation.com

Roof Books are distributed by
SMALL PRESS DISTRIBUTION
1341 Seventh Street • Berkeley, CA. 94710-1403.
Phone orders: 800-869-7553
spdbooks.org